THE POWER
OF BREATH

ૐ

July 2009

To Amani

with best wishes
Swami Saradananda

THE POWER OF BREATH

THE ART OF BREATHING WELL
FOR HARMONY, HAPPINESS AND HEALTH

SWAMI SARADANANDA

DUNCAN BAIRD PUBLISHERS

LONDON

THE POWER OF BREATH
Swami Saradananda

First published in the United Kingdom and Ireland in 2009 by
Duncan Baird Publishers Ltd
Sixth Floor
Castle House
75–76 Wells Street
London W1T 3QH

Conceived, created and designed by
Duncan Baird Publishers

Managing Editor: Kirty Topiwala
Editor: Susannah Marriott
Editorial Assistant: Duncan Carson
Managing Designer: Manisha Patel
Designer: Saskia Janssen
Commissioned Photography: Jules Selmes
Illustrator: Lydia Hess

British Library Cataloguing-in-Publication Data:
A CIP record for this book is available from the British Library

ISBN: 978-1-84483-789-2
10 9 8 7 6 5 4 3 2 1

Typeset in Spectrum MT
Colour reproduction by Colourscan, Singapore
Printed in Singapore by Imago

Publisher's note: The information in this book is not intended as a substitute for professional
medical advice and treatment. If you are pregnant or are suffering from any medical
conditions or health problems, it is recommended that you consult a medical professional
before following any of the advice or practice suggested in this book. Duncan Baird
Publishers, or any other persons who have been involved in working on this publication,
cannot accept responsibility for any injuries or damage incurred as a result of following the
information, exercises or therapeutic techniques contained in this book.

This book is dedicated to Swami Vishnu-devananda.
In addition to being my spiritual teacher and mentor,
he was a great master of pranayama.

*"And the Lord God formed man of the dust of the ground,
and breathed into his nostrils the breath of life;
and man became a living soul."*

Genesis, 2.7

CONTENTS

INTRODUCTION

Learning to breathe well is one of the most powerful ways to revitalize your body, mind and emotions. The benefits of breathing exercises are far-reaching. By maximizing your intake of oxygen and ridding your body of waste products, they boost every body system, helping you to feel and look both more vibrant and more relaxed, and to maintain a calm mind at times of tension. But the breathing exercises in this book offer more than this – they give you the tools and insight you need to access your life-force. Yoga philosophy teaches that your breath is the physical manifestation of the vital energy that gives you the ability to live and breathe, move about and function in the world. It is this life-force that allows you to think, digest food, hear sounds, laugh, sneeze and carry out the numerous activities you engage in at any moment, both consciously and unconsciously. This vital energy, which animates every being, is described in many Eastern philosophies, and in India is known as *prana*. Though not material in nature, prana flows through every part of your body, interpenetrating each cell like water filling a sponge.

The exercises in this book help you to make more efficient use of your prana, which has five functions, each one described as a different type of energy (*see right*). Each main chapter is dedicated to one of these five forms

BREATHING FOR LIFE

The exercises in this book will enhance your vigour and well-being, but for maximum benefit, try to back them up with a healthy lifestyle. This includes eating more fruit, vegetables and wholegrains, exercising most days and giving up negative indulgences, such as smoking. In these pages, you will find boxes offering breathing tips to make your work and home life more healthy. One of the best is simply to watch your breath through the day and take a few deep breaths, especially when you feel tense. Notice the effects on your mind, mood and body.

of prana, and offers exercises to enhance, expand and express them. When all five energies are vibrant and balanced, health and vitality follow.

PRANA (chapter 2, *see pages 38–61*) is the first of the five forms of prana (sharing its name), governing inhalations. This is your vitalizing breath – the dynamic force that enables you to take in all forms of energy.

SAMANA (chapter 3, *see pages 62–81*) is the second form of vital energy and processes the oxygen entering your lungs. This nourishing breath enables you to digest food and to understand thoughts and feelings.

VYANA (chapter 4, *see pages 82–103*) is the third form of vital energy and governs your circulation and the distribution of oxygen in your body. This is your expansive breath that distributes vital nourishment and equips you to expand into the world.

APANA (chapter 5, *see pages 104–27*) is the fourth form of vital energy and oversees exhalation and the release of carbon dioxide. As well as being a cleansing breath, it is the expelling force by which a child is born.

UDANA (chapter 6, *see pages 128–47*) is the fifth and final form of vital energy. It accompanies apana when you exhale, enabling your energy to "rise up" and find expression. This expressive breath gives you the energy you need to find a voice and turn your thoughts into action.

Whether you are new to breathing techniques or an experienced practitioner, it is best to begin by reading chapter 1, which outlines the benefits of breathwork, explains its theory and sets out techniques for cleansing your respiratory system and the basics of sitting to practise.

I hope this book will inspire you to try breath-enhancement techniques – they are a perfect addition to a detox, healthy eating campaign or exercise regime, and can help to counter problems associated with busy lifestyles. But I also hope that as the exercises put you in touch with your energetic core, you experience a profound understanding – that your ever-present breath connects you to a power far greater than yourself.

THE IMPORTANCE OF
BREATHING WELL

Of all the necessities in life, breathing is your most immediate. If you are a reasonably healthy person, you can probably go for about six weeks without food and for a few days without water. But without breathing, you would not survive for more than a few minutes.

Your breath is your most intimate companion on your journey through life. You began to breathe just a moment after you were born and some day you will "expire" with your very last exhalation. In between, your breath is with you wherever you go. Your breath is nearer to you than anything else, and dearer to you than your wealth and the people you love the most — for if you lose your breath, you lose everything. And yet, like most people, you probably rarely, if ever, think about how, or even why, you breathe.

Although no one can survive without breathing, many people manage to live a good portion of their lives without breathing properly. In the 30 years that I have been teaching yoga and meditation, I have found that even the most dedicated yogis often lack the insight, as well as the tools, to efficiently manage their breathing. The stressful pace of modern life together with sedentary jobs and leisure pursuits contribute to unhealthy breathing habits by creating tension in your body that inhibits the full expansion of your chest. But poor respiratory habits can take a heavy toll on your physical, mental and emotional health and happiness — viruses and bacteria thrive, for example, when your body is oxygen-deprived from not breathing properly. Shallow breathing also contributes to many chronic stress-related health conditions.

If you work in an office, take a look around you. Or do so next time you are sitting on a bus or a train. Notice how many people are only "half-breathing" — their inhalations are so shallow that their chests barely expand as they breathe in. You may not be able to see any movement at all. Notice, too, how these people only breathe out halfway, as it actually

BENEFITS OF BETTER BREATHING

Good breathing is healthy breathing – it helps to maintain and improve both your general physical health and your mental and emotional well-being in the following ways:

• *Boosts your energy and stamina.*
• *Counters tiredness and can reduce your need for sleep.*
• *Relieves tension in your body and enhances your ability to deal with pressure and stress.*
• *Brings a sheen of vitality to your complexion and eyes.*
• *Boosts your immunity and releases chemicals that promote healing.*
• *Increases your powers of concentration and ability to think clearly.*
• *Brings calmness and mastery of your emotions.*
• *Maximizes your verbal delivery by strengthening your voice and clarifying your thinking.*

takes more strength to breathe out properly than to breathe in fully. An asthmatic attack is an extreme example of this type of breathing. The sufferer tries to pull in much-needed oxygen-rich air, but since he or she finds it hard to exhale, his or her lungs are already filled with stale air and there is simply no room for fresh air. You need to breathe out properly before you can breathe in fully. For this reason, many of the exercises in this book emphasize exhalation. This is also why nature forces you to deflate your lungs by yawning or sighing when you are exhausted or bored – to force you to bring in fresh oxygen and revitalizing energy.

Carefully controlling your breath helps you to lead a fuller life by ridding your body of waste products and maximizing oxygen intake. It also relieves the symptoms of anxiety – such as a furrowed brow, tight shoulders and stomach cramps – and can calm your mind and improve your mood. As you practise the breathing exercises in this book, you will notice that you think more clearly, act with greater determination and are less carried away by your emotions.

THE BODY-BREATH-MIND CONNECTION

Your breath is the interface between your body and your mind. Every thought you have, action you take and emotion you experience influences your breathing – for example, excitement might speed your breathing to prepare your body to take action, or a surprise might cause you to inhale sharply to supply your brain with oxygen, promoting quick thinking.

When I teach breathing exercises, I often begin by demonstrating this intimate body-breath-mind connection. I ask students to close their eyes and count while I tap on a table. I begin by tapping slowly and loudly. Then I make the taps more irregular and softer. Most students hold their breath as they try to concentrate, without even being aware of it. Such a reaction is common even in the animal world. Watch how a cat, intent on catching a bird, stays perfectly still. The cat's concentration is so complete that he or she barely breathes. We understand this mind-breath-body connection as children. If a two-year-old were to find you breathing irregularly or fast, he or she would ask, "What's wrong?" This is not something that is taught: we all know it instinctively. By practising breathing exercises you can consciously make use of this instinctive knowledge and come to understand how powerfully your breathing influences your quality of mind and body. And because your body is a living system that constantly recreates itself, by practising breathing exercises you can voluntarily exert control to change unhealthy patterns of breathing, thinking and acting. For example, consciously slowing and deepening your breathing can help you to focus and act calmly under duress.

If you practise yoga, you are already retuning your body-breath-mind connection when you do breathing exercises called *pranayama*, a Sanskrit word meaning "control of the prana". Prana is the energy that animates you, and yogis regard breath as its physical manifestation. The exercises in this book help you to see how prana flows through you and how you can control it to enhance your physical, mental and emotional well-being.

UNDERSTANDING YOUR BREATH

Before beginning any practical breathing exercises, it is useful to familiarize yourself with the three elements that make up a single breath and their relative importance in your breathing practice. These are inhalation, exhalation and the transition between these two actions, known as retention. Exhalation is the focus of most breathing exercises.

Inhalation

As your lungs take in air, oxygen passes into your body, providing it with one of the essential ingredients of life. The inward flow of air into your lungs is more or less automatic: once you exhale, inhalation effortlessly follows. For this reason, the in-breath is not emphasized in many of the exercises in this book.

Exhalation

The outward flow of air from your lungs expels gaseous waste products, such as carbon dioxide, from your body – your lungs therefore act as an organ of excretion. Yogis believe that exhalation also eliminates impurities from the mind, and that if you suffer from shortness of breath

WHY QUIT SMOKING?

Smoking tobacco harms every organ in the body, but is particularly deadly for the organs of respiration – the lungs – and increases your risk of dying from lung disease ten-fold. The breathing exercises in this book will not make you stop smoking. However, if you would like to stop, they can offer some powerful assistance. Breathing exercises cleanse your respiratory system to make you feel revitalized. They can also strengthen your willpower by showing you that rather than giving something up, you are in fact giving yourself a gift – the joy that comes from breathing deeply again.

HOW BREATHING EXERCISES WORK

The following elements affect the outcome, or the physical and emotional effects, of any breathing exercise:

- *The length of the inhalation.*
- *The length of the exhalation (usually twice as long as the inhalation).*
- *How long you retain your breath after inhaling.*
- *The volume of air you inhale or exhale.*
- *The ratio of each part of your breath — the inhalation, exhalation and retention — to the other parts.*
- *Where in your body you focus your thoughts — for example, your heart or your navel.*
- *The number of times you repeat an exercise or a cycle of breaths.*

or cannot exhale completely, toxins will accumulate in your body which can negatively affect your mind. Exhaling also helps your mind and body adjust to change. For example, if you jump into a shower that is much colder than expected, you are likely to inhale sharply.

Retention

The absence of either inhalation or exhalation is known as retention, the transition between the two actions. When you inhale and hold your breath, the rate of gaseous exchange in your lungs goes up as a result of the increase in pressure (*see pages 20–21*). This means that more oxygen passes from your lungs into your bloodstream. At the same time, more carbon dioxide and other gaseous waste products pass from your blood into your lungs, ready to be eliminated with your exhalation. The pause made by your out-breath, as it stops for a moment en route to becoming your in-breath, is technically also a retention. This portion of your breath is rarely noticed, but it is actually deeply calming and is employed in some of the breathing exercises in this book.

CHAPTER 1

EXPLORING YOUR BREATH

Before you begin to explore the breathing exercises in this book, it is useful to understand how your respiratory system actually works. On the following pages you will learn about its anatomy – its physical structure – and its physiology – what happens when air passes into your lungs and out again. There are also exercises to help you check whether you are using your lungs and nasal passages to their best advantage.

The chapter then takes you deeper into the art of breathing as it reveals the anatomy of your subtle energy system and explains how physical breathing exercises manipulate the five energies within your body, collectively known in Indian yoga philosophy as *prana*. There are practical exercises here, too, to cleanse your energy system. After reading this chapter you will gain an understanding of how your breath underpins your physical, mental and emotional well-being, and be equipped with the tools to begin changing any unhealthy patterns.

Finally, this chapter presents all the information you need on the practical aspects of breathing, including where to practise, what to wear and how to sit comfortably to begin.

HOW YOUR BREATH WORKS

Your respiratory system stretches from your nose to your lungs, encompassing your nasal passages and sinus cavities, the back of your throat (pharynx), and your voice box (larynx), windpipe (trachea), bronchial tubes and lungs. It serves two life-giving purposes – bringing oxygen into your body and releasing waste matter – and enables a uniquely human quality, your ability to speak.

Each time you inhale, your respiratory system fulfils its first function, bringing atmospheric air into your lungs. The oxygen within this air is absorbed into your bloodstream and then transported to every cell in your body. Without this oxygen, your cells would die in a few minutes. The second task of your respiratory system is cleansing. Each time you exhale, you release gaseous waste matter from your body – mainly by-products of metabolism. As you breathe out, air passes over your vocal cords, allowing you to express yourself through your own unique sound. In no other body system does the outside environment, with all its germs and pollution, have so much contact with your sterile inner regions.

Your nose and sinuses
The nose is the first part of your body to engage with breathing and it also plays a important protective role in your survival. As the seat of your olfactory mechanism – your most primitive sense, smell – it warns you of impending danger. Nature has also designed it as the ideal mechanism for filtering incoming air to protect the delicate lining of your lungs. Each nostril leads to an air passage separated by a bony structure made of cartilage called the septum. The internal portion of your nostrils is lined with microscopic hairs, known as cilia. When you breathe through your nose, these filters cleanse the air you inhale of dust, pollen, airborne germs and pollution. If you breathe through your mouth, without these filters, you may suffer a dry mouth, sore throat or

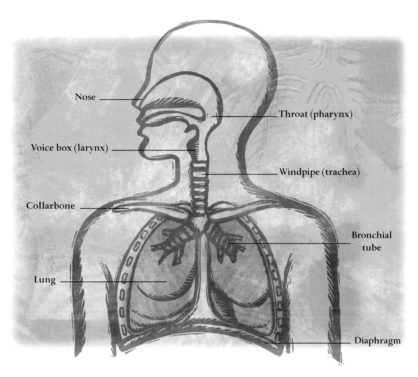

Nose

Throat (pharynx)

Voice box (larynx)

Windpipe (trachea)

Collarbone

Bronchial tube

Lung

Diaphragm

catch a cold as a result. You should therefore only breathe through your mouth when a cold obstructs your nostrils, or when you need more air than your nostrils can comfortably inhale, such as when running.

Breathing through your nose also protects your respiratory system by humidifying the incoming air to keep the mucus membranes lining your nose, throat and respiratory passages moist. They then form a second line of defence, trapping dust and bacteria on their sticky surfaces. Mouth-breathing dries out the mucus membranes, making them less effective. Breathing through your nose also allows your nasal cavities and sinuses to bring the air you inhale to body temperature, as cold air irritates the respiratory system. Regular nose-breathing clears your sinuses, the internal cavities behind your cheekbones and forehead. You may only become aware of them when they are inflamed by a cold or hayfever, but clear sinuses promote good air circulation, bringing a feeling of lightness and freedom from headaches. They also add resonance to your voice.

Your lungs, throat and chest

After air has entered your nasal passages, it moves down the back of your throat and past your larynx. This "voice box" contains your vocal cords and muscles that work together to produce sound. Air then descends into your trachea, or windpipe, which divides into two bronchial tubes. From here on, your respiratory system resembles two bunches of grapes – each bronchial tube sub-divides, becoming smaller and smaller until the passages consist of no more than a single layer of cells. Each passage ends in a tiny air sac, or alveolus. Your lungs are composed of millions of these microscopic, grape-like sacs. The membrane enclosing each one comprises a thin layer of cells surrounded by a network of capillaries (small blood vessels). Here, the all-important gaseous exchange takes place (*see below*).

Your lungs and heart are enclosed by your ribcage, which is moved by intercostal muscles between your ribs. These muscles expand your ribs as you inhale and draw them closer as you exhale. At the floor of your chest cavity is a flat muscle, the diaphragm, which separates it from your abdominal cavity. As your diaphragm expands downward, it creates a vacuum in your chest cavity. Air rushes in to fill the vacuum, causing you to inhale. Once your diaphragm relaxes, it contracts and moves upward, pushing air out of your lungs, making you exhale. On moving downward, your diaphragm expands into your abdominal cavity, causing your abdomen to swell gently if you are breathing correctly. As you exhale, your abdomen contracts. To see this natural breathing in action, watch a baby's tummy moving in and out as he or she sleeps.

Gaseous exchange

The average adult at rest breathes 15–18 times per minute. With each inhalation, you draw approximately half a litre (1.75 pints) of air into your lungs. Every time you exhale, an equal amount of air is expelled.

The air you inhale comprises about 79 percent nitrogen, 20 percent oxygen and 0.04 percent carbon dioxide, with traces of other gases and water vapour. The air you exhale contains the same amount of nitrogen, but the oxygen content falls to 16 percent and the carbon dioxide rises to 4 percent, so the most significant change between breathing in and out is the exchange of 4 percent oxygen for 4 percent carbon dioxide.

Oxygen from the air you inhale passes into your capillaries (small blood vessels) through the thin porous membranes of your alveoli, or tiny air sacs. Simultaneously, carbon dioxide from the blood moves into the air sacs to be breathed out. After your blood has been oxygenated in your lungs, it travels to your heart and is pumped around your body, delivering oxygen and nutrients to every cell, where it picks up the gaseous waste products of metabolism, including carbon dioxide, and takes them to your lungs, ready to be exhaled.

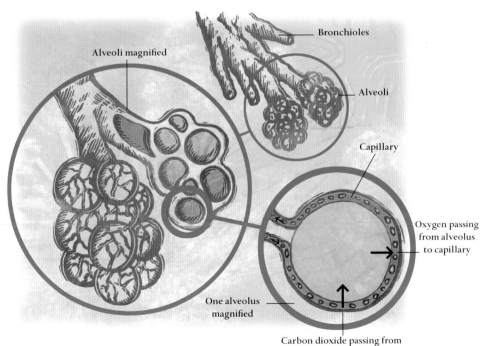

YOUR ENERGETIC BREATH

A traditional Indian depiction of the body showing
some of the subtle energy channels or nadis,
and the key chakras (see pages 24—5).

What powers the vital processes that bring your physical body alive, giving it the dynamism to move and breathe? What regulates your senses and the way you perceive, think and act? Ancient yoga texts tell us it is a subtle energy known as *prana*. This is not physical energy — prana is quite different from the electrical impulses in your nervous system — yet it flows through your body and manifests itself through your breath. By changing your breathing, you can direct this vital energy force.

The Sanskrit word *prana* is usually translated as "vital air", "life-force" or "vital energy", but none of these descriptions really explain it. We can't translate the word into English, or any Western language, because until recently our culture lacked the concept. The Chinese word *chi* (as in tai chi) or the Japanese word *ki* (as in reiki) are exact translations. People who practise acupuncture, reflexology and most martial arts understand and work with prana. Your prana is divided into five categories each "governing" aspects of your body, mind and breath (*see pages 8–9*). Each main chapter of this book reveals how one of them works.

Your energy highway

Prana flows through your body in subtle energy channels called *nadis*. Approximately 72,000 criss-cross your body (*see image opposite*) – you might like to think of them as roads on an energy highway system. The traffic on the roads is your prana. When traffic flows freely the system works well, but if a nadi becomes blocked, the flow of prana to that region of the body is reduced or even cut off. Without the nourishment of vital energy, that part of the body may weaken or become sick. For your body to be vibrantly healthy, an unimpeded flow of prana is necessary. One way to encourage this is to practise breathing exercises.

The main nadis

Of your 72,000 energy lines, three are of particular interest in our exploration of breathing. The *ida* channel flows to the left of your spine, the *pingala* to the right, and the central channel, which approximates your spine, is known as the *sushumna*. The left and right channels are associated with qualities of mind (*see pages 54–7*), and when your breath flows through one of these channels it develops these qualities in you. Various breathing exercises can guide your breath through the left and right channels. The only time your breath flows evenly is during meditation, when it enters the central energy channel and both sides of your brain are balanced. In order to achieve a state of meditation, ancient yogis developed breathing exercises referred to as *pranayama*. Practising pranayama is one of the main disciplines within hatha yoga (*see page 156*).

Chakra energy centres

The point where two or more nadis meet forms a junction of energy known as a *chakra*, Sanskrit for "wheel". You might like to visualize these whirling balls of energy as a multi-dimensional telephone exchange where numerous wires feed in and distribute vast amounts of information. The more nadis that intersect, the more likely your energy highway is to become blocked, which is why many breathing techniques aim to clear energy junctions so that prana can flow freely again.

There are seven major chakras on the sushumna, your central energy channel: around the crown of your head, around your forehead, throat, heart, solar plexus, lower abdomen and around the base of your spine. Each chakra governs a different sense, type of emotion and quality of mind and body function (*see opposite*). As energy passes up through the chakras in your energetic system, it becomes more rarified.

● SAHASRARA CHAKRA

● AJNA CHAKRA

● VISHUDDHA CHAKRA

● ANAHATA CHAKRA

● MANIPURA CHAKRA

● SWADHISTHANA CHAKRA

● MULADHARA CHAKRA

THE SEVEN MAJOR CHAKRAS

SAHASRARA CHAKRA, at the crown of your head, is where you receive the inspiration to venture beyond self-defined limitations. Focusing breathing exercises on this chakra helps you to develop a connection with the divine and enhances your sense of wonder.

AJNA CHAKRA, at the centre of your forehead, lies beyond the five elements and your senses, and is the seat of intuition and imagination. Focusing breathing exercises on this chakra enhances understanding and wisdom and helps you to develop a purpose in life.

VISHUDDHA CHAKRA, at your throat, is associated with the element space, or ether, and your sense of hearing. It is your energetic centre of communication. Focusing breathing exercises on this chakra brings about calmness and enhances communication skills.

ANAHATA CHAKRA, around your heart, is associated with the element air, your sense of touch and love. Focusing breathing exercises on this chakra helps you to develop compassion and forgiveness.

MANIPURA CHAKRA, around your solar plexus, is associated with the element fire and your sense of sight. It is your body's power centre and the site of your digestive fire (*see page 72*). Focusing breathing exercises on this chakra helps you to harness willpower and realize your ambitions.

SWADHISTHANA CHAKRA, sited around your lower abdomen, is associated with the water element and your sense of taste. This chakra embodies creative energy and is the seat of your sexuality, plans and desire. Focusing breathing exercises on this chakra helps you to go with the flow and taste all that life has to offer.

MULADHARA CHAKRA, at the base of your spine, is associated with the earth element and your sense of smell. This is the seat of a vast potential energy known as *kundalini*, said to be lying dormant, waiting to be awakened. Focusing breathing exercises on this chakra helps you to put down roots and develop steadiness of mind.

BREATHING FOR STRESS-RELIEF

To understand the connection between breathing and stress, when you are next under pressure or feel worried, watch how your muscles tighten and your breathing speeds up and becomes increasingly shallow. This is an instinctive response known as the "fight-or-flight" mechanism, which prepares your body to face physical dangers by priming your muscles to defend yourself or to run away. The pressures of modern life can trigger this response many times during a typical day – when you are stuck in traffic, or faced with impossible deadlines or the demands of a constantly ringing phone. But it is not usually possible to run away from a traffic jam, nor is it a good idea to fight with your boss or your cellphone! Instead, you may find yourself relieving your tension in self-destructive ways – by shouting, crying or reaching for a cigarette. A more healthy response would be to take some deep breaths. Breathing deeply is the simplest antidote to the fight-or-flight response, returning your body systems to a more restful state. But if you are unaccustomed to breathing deeply when unstressed, you may find that deep, full breathing is virtually impossible in stressful situations. Use the exercise opposite to introduce yourself to the de-stressing benefits of deeper breathing.

As well as easing physical tension, deep breathing increases clarity of thought and helps to overcome the noise of a busy mind. It promotes a sense of groundedness in challenging situations and enables you to react calmly to difficult people. Ancient yoga texts describe this effect using the analogy of a lake or an ocean. Rough weather churns up sediment, making the water murky. But as the wind dies down, the mud gradually settles and the water becomes clear. Similarly, the faster you breathe, the more distracting thoughts and emotions churn up your mind. As you relax into deep, long breaths, your thinking becomes clearer and your mind more lucid. This enhances your inner resilience and mental flexibility, which leads to a feeling of calmness and empowerment.

WATCHING YOUR BREATH

This exercise calms your mind in stressful situations. Start by sitting comfortably in one of the positions recommended on pages 34–7, then close your eyes and just watch your breathing rising and falling. Do not do anything else, and do not try to change or consciously slow your breathing. When you feel ready, begin step 1, below.

1 Sit with your back straight and your head upright. Gently seal your lips and inhale though your nose. Feel the air entering your nostrils and moving past the back of your throat. Picture it moving down your trachea, or windpipe, into your bronchial tubes and then entering and filling your lungs.

2 At the end of the in-breath, notice a momentary halt in your breathing as your in-breath "turns around" to transform itself into your out-breath.

3 As you exhale through your nose, be aware of your lungs emptying themselves of air. Visualize your breath moving up past your throat and out through your nostrils.

4 Feel a breeze on your upper lip at the end of the out-breath. Then notice the slight pause as your out-breath stops for a moment before becoming the next in-breath.

5 Repeat, but as you take each in-breath, visualize yourself joyously drawing in life-energy. On the exhalations consciously release any pent-up emotions, letting them go as you breathe out impurities, including carbon dioxide.

6 Keep watching and listening to your breath, noticing that as it becomes calmer and slower, your mind, too, feels calmer and slower.

7 Try to sit for 10–20 minutes with your mind completely focused on your breath. Whenever your mind drifts off, bring your thoughts back to your breath. Lastly, stand up, stretch and notice how much calmer you feel.

ASSESSING YOUR BREATH

Before beginning the exercise-based chapters in this book (*see chapters 2–6*), it is important to analyze your current breathing habits by asking yourself the four questions that follow. They will help you to identify some of the most common bad breathing habits, and then offer techniques to help you begin to undo the patterns. Once you have mastered the solutions and feel that you are breathing more deeply and easily, feel free to begin the practical breathing exercises in this chapter and chapter 2.

1   Do you breathe through your nose or your mouth?
Unless you have a cold or are engaged in vigorous exercise, always try to breathe through your nose. This allows the filters in your respiratory system to cleanse the air you inhale of any bacteria and impurities and it also helps to keep your sinuses healthy (*see page 19*). Some breathing practitioners, including therapists of the Buteyko method (*see page 157*), suggest taping your mouth shut for a short period to check whether you breathe through your nose or mouth. If you feel comfortable trying this, place 2–3 inches (5–8 cm) of paper surgical tape (from a pharmacy) vertically over your lips, from top to bottom and press lightly to secure. For 15–30 minutes, engage in silent activities, such as chopping vegetables, checking your emails or watching television.

CAUTION: Remove the tape from your mouth immediately if you feel at all distressed. Avoid this exercise if you have a cold or a blocked nose, have drunk alcohol or taken sleeping tablets, sedatives or muscle relaxants. Never tape a child's mouth shut.

SOLUTION: If, after trying out the diagnostic technique above, you do not feel comfortable breathing through your nose, then practise one of the cleansing exercises on pages 31–2, which will help to cleanse and clear your nasal passages and can help you to break the habit of breathing through your mouth.

SOLVING COMMON OBSTACLES TO GOOD BREATHING

- *Blocked nose and/or sinuses (once your cold has passed, see question 1).*
- *Tightness in chest (see question 3).*
- *Tight-fitting clothing (remove restrictive garments, then see questions 2 and 3).*
- *Full stomach/intestinal bloating (wait 2–3 hours after eating, then answer questions 1–4).*
- *Poor posture (see question 4).*
- *Excessive nervous tension (try Watching Your Breath, see page 27, before answering all four diagnostic questions).*

2   Is your breathing shallow or deep?

Most people breathe shallowly, using only the upper portion of their lungs. To assess the depth of your breathing, lie on your back on a firm surface (not a bed or soft furniture). Put a cushion under your head or neck. Separate your legs, relax your feet and shake out your shoulders. Gently roll your head from side to side, then return it to centre. Rest your palms around your navel and take long, slow breaths, feeling your abdomen rise with each inhalation and fall with each exhalation. Try to draw air into the lowest portion of your lungs, expanding your abdomen.

SOLUTION: If you cannot feel your abdomen moving, place a few books on it. Then relax your arms on the floor at about 45 degrees from your body with your palms facing upward and fingers gently curled. Keeping your head on the ground, open your eyes and look forward. When you breathe deeply, the books will rise as you inhale and drop as you exhale. With a child, substitute a doll or soft toy for books and ask the child to use his or her breath to give it a ride.

3   Do you use a small portion of your lungs or their full capacity?

After perfecting deep abdominal breathing (*see above*), see if you are using your full lung capacity. Sit cross-legged on the floor or on a straight-backed chair with your feet flat on the floor. Straighten your back, lift

your breastbone and relax your shoulders. Place one hand near your navel and the other on the bottom of your ribcage (above your waist). Notice your hands moving – as you inhale, your lower hand should move first, then your upper hand. This should reverse on the exhalation. If your hands don't move, or move only slightly as you inhale, then you are not using your lungs fully.

SOLUTION: To learn to use them more fully, sit with your hands placed as before, close your eyes and visualize your lungs as long, skinny balloons. As you inhale, picture yourself taking a deep breath that fills the bottom of the balloons, then imagine the middle of the balloons inflating; finally fill the top with air. Feel first your abdomen, then your ribcage and finally your upper chest expand. As you exhale, feel the process reversing. This technique may take some days to master.

4   Do you hunch your shoulders?

Next time you climb a flight of stairs, observe your breath and notice how soon you start to pant. Next, bring your awareness to your shoulder blades. Are they wide apart? This rounds your back and shoulders, causing your chest to cave in, which makes deep breathing difficult.

SOLUTION: If you do hunch your shoulders, press your shoulder blades together and draw them toward your waist. This frees your abdomen of unnecessary pressure and lets your diaphragm move easily, instantly allowing you to breathe more deeply. Now tune your breath and footsteps to each other. Inhale on the first two steps and exhale on the next two. Breathing rhythmically expels more carbon dioxide, enabling your lungs to take in a more generous supply of oxygen.

CLEANSING YOUR RESPIRATORY SYSTEM

The first goal of breathing exercises is to cleanse and strengthen your respiratory system. The exercises here and on page 32 are good ways to cleanse your nasal passages and sinus cavities before starting any other breathing exercise.

Hold and blow

Practitioners of the Buteyko method (*see page 157*) recommend practising the following cleansing method 3–5 times daily. Keeping your mouth closed, simply breathe in through your nose, then out. Now pinch your nostrils closed. Imagine trying to blow your nose and maintain a gentle pressure for about 5 seconds, with your nose and mouth closed. Release your nostrils and very gently breathe in through your nose.

Neti cleansing

Many people like to cleanse the nasal passages and sinuses with a salt-water solution after brushing their teeth in the morning. This removes dust, pollen and excess mucus and can help if you have asthma, allergies or respiratory problems. You can buy neti pots from health-food shops, pharmacies or online. Practise in front of a mirror so that you can see your nostrils.

Dissolve ½ teaspoon of fine sea-salt into a cup of lukewarm water and then pour it into the neti pot. Leaning over a sink, inhale and hold your breath, making sure that you keep your mouth closed. Tighten the back of your throat as if to gargle. Tilt your head left and slowly pour the water into your right nostril. Let gravity drain the water out through your left nostril. Do not inhale. Blow your nose and repeat the process on the left nostril, this time tilting your head to the right.

PURIFYING BREATH
KAPALABHATI

This breathing technique cleanses your respiratory system while strengthening and increasing your lung capacity. With regular practice, it can purify your entire system so thoroughly that your face starts to shine with good health and inner radiance (the Sanskrit word *kapala* means "skull" and *bhati* means "shining"). Practise this purifying breath before you begin other breathing exercises. If you find the mechanics of the "pumping" difficult to grasp, seek out the guidance of an experienced yoga teacher to practise with.

1 Begin sitting with your back straight and your head erect, preferably in a cross-legged position (*see pages 35–7*). Take 2–3 deep breaths in and out through your nose.

2 Inhale, and begin the rhythmic pumping by contracting your abdominal muscles quickly and then immediately releasing them – about 20–25 times. Contracting quickly causes your diaphragm to move up into your thoracic cavity, emptying the stale air from your lungs and forcefully pushing it out of your nostrils. Make every exhalation brief, active and audible. After each forceful exhalation, immediately relax your abdominal muscles – inhalation will then take place automatically. Do not forcefully inhale, simply allow your lungs to open and fill with fresh air. Your inhalation is always best when it is passive and silent.

3 After completing approximately 20–25 pumpings, end on an exhalation and then take 2–3 deep breaths to bring your breathing back to normal. This completes one round.

4 Start by trying to do 2–3 rounds (of 20–25 pumpings each) before you practise other breathing exercises, gradually increasing the number of abdominal pumps in each round to 30–50, and then relax.

CAUTION: DO NOT PRACTISE DURING PREGNANCY.

PREPARING FOR BREATHING

To derive optimum benefit from breathing exercises, it is best to establish a routine for your practice and to set aside a specific time each day. The best times are at sunrise, sunset and noon, when your breath is thought to be more evenly balanced between your right and left energy channels (*see page 23*). Practising as the sun is rising brings added benefit, although this may be easier in the winter than in summer.

When to practise
Practising breathing first thing in the morning leaves you feeling more mentally balanced and better equipped emotionally to face a busy day. Alternatively, you may choose to practise at lunchtime. If you practise after work, do so before eating dinner or wait at least 2–3 hours after eating. Never practise breathing exercises on a full stomach.

Set aside a time for practice when distractions are minimal – if you are a parent, perhaps in the morning after delivering children to school, or in the evening after they have gone to bed. Try not to practise within 2 hours of your own bedtime because you may find that breathing exercises tend to be invigorating. Also, plan your practice for a time when you can turn off your phones, television and other electronic distractions.

Where to practise
Whenever possible, select a peaceful place outdoors, such as a quiet spot in a park or a garden. It is always best to practise in nature, especially near moving water. In India, yogis have been practising breathing exercises on the banks of the Ganges river for thousands of years. If you live in a city or if the weather makes a natural venue difficult, then practise in a well-ventilated room. Make sure the room is not too warm, because breathing exercises tend to increase your body temperature. Dress in loose-fitting clothing, preferably made from natural fibres.

THE ART OF SITTING

Your lungs need space to be able to expand fully in breathing exercises. Sitting with your spine perpendicular to the ground, your head upright and shoulders relaxed gives them that space. It also aids concentration and calmness, while promoting energy flow throughout your body. The steadier your sitting pose, the more focused, calm and energized you'll feel. To begin your practice, choose whichever sitting pose feels most comfortable from those shown on the following pages, and vary them as you become more accomplished. Try to remember that perfect posture is effortless – if you ever feel any tension in your body while you are sitting to practise breathing exercises, stretch out your legs and adopt a more comfortable pose. It is important not to force your legs (or any other part of your body) into painful positions.

Sitting on a chair

Try to sit on the floor to practise breathing exercises, but if you find this very uncomfortable, sit on a straight-backed chair. Avoid upholstered chairs – on soft surfaces it is difficult to keep your back straight. Place your feet flat on the floor (or on a folded blanket) and let this firm contact "ground" your body and mind. Try to resist the temptation to cross your legs or ankles, or to lean against the back of the chair. Rest your hands on your thighs with palms facing upward or in Chin Mudra (*see below*).

POSITIONING YOUR HANDS

During breathing exercises, either rest your hands on your knees with your palms facing upward, or place them in the classical yoga hand position for breathing exercises, known as Chin Mudra (see left). Simply join the tips of your thumb and forefinger on each hand and rest the backs of your hands on your knees.

TAILOR POSE
SUKHASANA

This easy cross-legged pose provides a firm base for your spine to lengthen out of and encourages your mind to stay focused. With practice, tightness in your hips will lessen and your lower-back muscles strengthen. Relax your eyes, whether they are open, closed or somewhere in between.

1 Sit on the floor with your legs crossed in front of you. Make sure your knees are no higher than your hips. If you are a beginner or your hips are stiff, sit on a cushion, yoga block or folded blanket. This lifts your buttocks and relieves tension in your lower back and hips (*see image A*).

2 Check your body to make sure that your back is straight, your shoulders are relaxed and your head is upright, with your chin parallel to the ground (*see image B*). Rest your hands on your knees, either with your palms facing upward or in Chin Mudra (*see opposite page, below*).

ADEPT'S POSE
SIDDHASANA

This sitting position is a little more difficult than Tailor Pose (*see page 35*), but easier than the Lotus Poses opposite.

1 Sit on the ground with your legs stretched forward. If you are a beginner or if you feel any stiffness in your lower back or hips, place a cushion beneath your buttocks.

2 Bend your left knee and place your left heel just in front of your pubic bone, as close to your body as possible.

3 Now fold in your right knee, placing your right heel directly in front of your left heel. Rest your hands on your knees either with your palms facing upward or in Chin Mudra (*see page 34*).

THUNDERBOLT POSE
VAJRASANA

This kneeling pose stimulates energy around your solar plexus. If you are uncomfortable with your weight on your heels, rest your buttocks on a low bench (available in yoga centres or online) as used in Zen meditation.

1 Kneel on a mat with knees and feet together (or slightly apart), and buttocks on your heels. Cushion aching ankles or feet with a rolled-up face cloth. Rest your hands on your thighs, palms facing upward or in Chin Mudra (*see page 34*).

2 Visualize your legs and feet growing roots into the earth, drawing up stability, strength and stillness.

HALF-LOTUS POSE
ARDHA PADMASANA

Though simpler than the full Lotus Pose (see below), this position brings many of the same benefits by stabilizing and grounding your body. Change over legs when you cross them each time you practise to stretch them both equally.

1 Sit on the ground with your legs crossed comfortably in front of you. Bend your right knee and gently place your right foot on your left thigh, with the sole of the foot facing upward.

2 Rest your hands on your knees, either with your palms facing upward or in Chin Mudra (*see page 34*).

LOTUS POSE
PADMASANA

This advanced pose provides a firm base for breathing exercises, but requires considerable hip flexibility. Try it if you can sit comfortably in Half-lotus Pose without forcing your legs. But avoid if you have knee problems or varicose veins.

1 Sit with legs crossed. Bend your right knee and place your right foot on your left thigh, as close to your trunk as you can, sole up. Guide your left foot onto your right thigh.

2 Check that both soles face up and your knees touch the ground. If not, return to Half-lotus Pose. Rest your hands on your knees, palms up or in Chin Mudra (*see page 34*).

CHAPTER 2

YOUR VITALIZING BREATH

UNDERSTANDING PRANA

The first of the five forms of prana — the energy, or driving force, behind all energy — that flows through your body is, rather confusingly, also known as prana. Yoga teachers will tell you that every time you breathe in, you draw in this vital energy along with the air you inhale. Just as you need physical oxygen to vitalize your body, you need prana to enliven your mind and emotions.

The region of the body most affected by prana energy

In the following pages, you will discover how this vitalizing prana breath enables you not only to inhale air into your lungs, but to take in stimuli of all forms — from sights, sounds and smells to feelings, ideas and knowledge. For prana provides the basic stimulus that sets all things in motion. In doing so, it enhances your appreciation of, and zest for, life, and opens your heart and mind to new possibilities of every kind — from your personal creativity and productivity at work to your relationships with others and your environment.

YOUR DYNAMIC LIFE-FORCE

If you imagine that your body is a factory, your prana is the person in charge. As the chief of the five forms of energy in your body, your incoming breath is responsible for authorizing all acquisitions and overseeing the intake of all raw materials. When prana stops doing its job, the factory closes down.

Prana is the root source of all the energy in the universe. Whether this energy manifests itself as heat, the sun, rushing water or the wind, all forces of nature are manifestations of prana. Within your body, the strongest influence of this vitalizing breath extends from your lungs and heart up to your nose. Prana endows your lungs with their ability to draw in all forms of prana, giving your eyes their energy to see, your ears their ability to hear and your mind its power to make sense of the world; prana nourishes your brain as it supervises the workings of your nervous system.

If you frequently feel stressed or exhausted, you may not be taking in enough prana. Alternatively, you may be wasting your prana, perhaps by overworking or allowing it to drain away as you spend long hours in front of a computer or a television, or sit in air-conditioned rooms or use a microwave. All of these activities deplete prana. Compare how tired and drained you feel in these situations with how energized you feel standing in a place rich in prana, such as near the ocean.

Ancient yoga texts state that the symptoms of any illness are the manifestation of a decreased flow of prana to particular parts of the body.

PREVENTING LOSS OF PRANA AT WORK

Help to stem the loss of prana caused by working at a computer by cultivating a cactus or a spider plant nearby, which produces oxygen and energizes stale air. Let it be a visual reminder to boost your prana by taking a break to practise breathing exercises.

WORKING WITH PRANA ENERGY

As you use the breathing exercises in this chapter, ask yourself the following questions. They can help you to see how you are depleting your prana and find ways in which you rebalance it.

- *Do I breathe deeply and fully, using my full lung capacity? (See page 29.)*
- *Do I nourish my body and mind with prana in the form of clean air, healthy food and stimulating ideas?*
- *Am I able to absorb the beauty around me? How does it strengthen me?*
- *Do I tend to "bite off more than I can chew"? Does this deplete my prana?*
- *Is my life chaotic? Is this because I am unable to direct my energy?*
- *Do I permit people to drain me emotionally? Or do I drain other people's prana by making unreasonable demands on them?*
- *Do I waste time by being unfocused? Or do I allow others to waste my time?*
- *Am I overly negative and self-critical? Is this because I allow people to deprive me of my independence and freewill?*

Although such a depletion is usually gradual, the effects of a sudden lack of prana can sometimes be obvious. If you experience a shock, for example, you may begin losing weight rapidly, see your hair turn grey overnight, or find that an internal organ ceases to function – for example in a heart attack.

Through practising the breathing exercises in this chapter, you can become conscious of the flow of prana within your body. By breathing with concerted awareness, you may find that you can extract more life-energy and deliberately direct it wherever it is required, whenever it is needed. As you become familiar with the exercises and practise them regularly, you may notice changes in the way your body functions and the fullness with which you live life. You may even notice your appearance changing, making you appear more alive, fresh-faced and youthful.

PRANA VISUALIZATION:
DRAWING IN PRANA

The breath-visualization exercise, opposite, focuses your awareness on the headquarters of the prana energy in your body. This is found at the "third eye" in the middle of your forehead. The "third eye" is another name for your ajna chakra (*see page 25*), the energy centre that manages your senses, your conscious and unconscious minds and your sense of self.

From this control centre at your brow, the propulsive energy of prana moves inward and downward to the bottom of your lungs, from where it acts as the main on-off switch that stimulates all your other subtle energies into action. Try to keep in mind the idea of inward-moving energy as you practise the exercise, opposite. You might like to picture prana as a welcoming figure within you, who opens a door and allows energy to enter every time you breathe in air, take a bite of food, listen to an idea or have a drink of water. Feel reassured that she will whisk the incoming energy to the proper processing area within your body, whether your lungs, stomach or mind, ready to be used appropriately.

You can practise the Prana Breathing exercise, opposite, anywhere and at any time, but it is particularly effective when you feel depleted of energy and would like to recharge your batteries. For a variation, combine this exercise with Alternate Nostril Breathing (*see page 55*).

HARNESSING PRANA

Have you ever had to tell someone something that was disagreeable, but necessary? Think of how you instinctively prepared yourself to do it. You probably took a deep breath, held it for a moment and then, with a deep sigh, thought, "OK, let me get this over with." If so, you were unconsciously harnessing prana. By holding your breath, you efficiently extracted an extra "jolt" of energy to help you to accomplish your unpleasant task.

PRANA BREATHING EXERCISE

Start by sitting comfortably, preferably with your legs crossed (*see pages 35–7*). Draw your shoulder blades down toward your waist to lift your breastbone and allow your ribcage to move freely as you breathe.

1 Sit with your back straight. Gently seal your lips and breathe through your nose. Bring your palms together and raise them over your head.

2 Inhale deeply through your nose, draw in as much air as possible. Open your eyes wide, bulge them out, and imagine drawing in light. Visualize yourself drawing in energy through your ears, your face and the top of your head.

3 When your lungs are full, hold your breath. Close your eyes and bring your awareness to the point between your eyebrows. Visualize the energy you inhaled forming a sphere of bright, concentrated light at the centre of your forehead. It may give off sparks or even lightning flashes. Retain your breath for as long as is comfortable.

4 As you exhale, watch the light dissolve into a sparkling shower of energy that invigorates you. Start with one breath and gradually build up to 10.

PRANA FABLE:
THE SWARM OF THE SENSES

"Prana burns as fire; he shines as the sun.
He is the bountiful rain-cloud, and blows as the wind.
He is the earth and the moon; he has form and no form; Prana is immortality."
Prasna Upanishad, 2.5

"Once upon a time, Prana was having an argument with the Mind and the Senses. Each of them claimed to be the most important part of the body, and they behaved like a swarm of angry bees, noisily competing for the body's attention. Prana warned the others, 'Don't be deluded – I am the one who keeps the body alive. I sustain life by dividing myself five-fold.' But, in their conceit, the Mind and the Senses refused to believe her. In an attempt to settle the dispute, they decided to try an experiment. Each of them in turn would leave the body and remain away for one year. On returning, they would all judge whose absence had had the greatest effect on the body.

Speech left first. When she returned she asked, 'How did you do without me?' The others replied that, though the body had been mute, they had all been fine. Next, Sight left for a year, and the body carried on, though it was blind. When Hearing left, the body was deaf, but nevertheless remained alive and healthy. Even when Mind left, the body survived, despite being unconscious.

Finally the time came for Prana to leave the body. As she began to make her departure, the Mind and all the Senses felt their energy ebbing away with her. They simply could not resist the force of Prana and were drawn to follow her, like a swarm of bees accompanying their queen out of the hive. As a result, the body began to die. Needless to say, the Mind and all the Senses apologized for their initial arrogance and begged Prana to stay. They agreed unanimously that Prana was truly the most important part of the body. "

Interpreting the tale

This story highlights the role prana plays in your body in endowing all your faculties with the energy they need to function. Without prana, your tongue cannot speak, your ears cannot hear, your eyes do not see and your mind cannot think. Without your life-force, you lack the energy to do anything. This goes against common-sense thinking, which holds that your senses are under the intelligent control of your mind. Actually, your mind and your senses are often quite out of control and lacking in discipline — your tongue, for example, often urges you to indulge your taste buds by treating them to their favourite flavours even after you have eaten more than enough, or your eyes and ears might tempt you to stay up late to watch the latest movie, although your reasoning mind tells you that you will regret it next morning, when you have to get up early for work.

If you want to be in control of your life, the key is to gain control of your prana. And if you want to control your prana, the best place to begin is by controlling your breath, because your breath is the most tangible manifestation of your prana. It is for this reason that yoga and many other forms of mind-body exercise, such as t'ai chi and chi gung, put so much emphasis on breathing exercises.

COPING WITH NEGATIVE EMOTIONS

"Equalize the out-going and in-coming breaths moving within your nostrils.
Control your senses, mind and intellect; have liberation as your supreme goal.
Be free from lust, fear and anger."
Bhagavad Gita, 5.27–28

How do you relieve tension when situations make you feel angry or frustrated? Do you shout, punch pillows or slam doors? Maybe you bottle up your feelings instead? All of these strategies drain you of prana, and when sustained over a period of time can contribute to chronic physical health conditions. And since they don't help you to address the root of the problem, they leave issues unresolved.

To deal with all negative emotions – but especially anger – in a more healthy way, stop what you are doing and take a few long, slow, deep breaths. Visualize yourself drawing in as much prana as possible alongside the air you inhale. This extra energy nourishes your mind, so that you can find a healthy outlet for your negative emotions. As the positive energy of all the vitalizing prana you have inhaled percolates through to your body, riding on the wave of your breath, it helps to relieve any physical symptoms of tension, too, such as knotted muscles. In this way, rather than allowing your negative emotions to control you, you use the strength of your vitalizing breath to control them.

To better understand the relationship between your breath, mind and emotions, try to practise being a "silent witness" for a few days. Watch yourself with an objective, non-judgmental attitude – with the same detached interest that you might observe a stranger in a café. Monitor yourself engaging in various activities – speaking to someone who is rude to you, giving an impromptu talk, reacting when your boss assigns you a distasteful task, sitting on a stalled train when you are late for an important appointment. If you start to get flustered or upset, switch on

COUNTING BACKWARD

Whenever you find yourself upset by the frustrations of day-to-day life, try this breath-counting exercise. Counting backward increases your concentration, which focuses your distracted mind and keeps you on a more even emotional keel. This in turn has a vitalizing effect on your body and mind. When you are full of positive prana, there is no space for anger or frustration.

1 Gently sealing your mouth and breathing through your nose, inhale for a count of 4, then exhale for a count of 4.

2 Now repeat, but counting backward – inhale, three, two, one; exhale, three, two, one. Take at least 10 deep breaths in and out, then judge whether you need to take 10 more.

3 As you regulate your breath, notice what happens to your emotions – do you feel calmer or less bothered? Watch what is happening to your body, too – are your shoulders and neck muscles relaxing or your fists uncurling?

your observing mind. Examine your reactions and mental behaviour, make a note of how much or how little you seem to be controlled by your emotions, and scan your body for tension. Then, examine the state of your breath. Is it fast or slow, deep or shallow, or are you so tense that you are holding your breath? Now begin to breathe consciously. Either use the Counting Backward exercise above or just try to take long, slow, deep in-breaths and then exhale fully, using every part of your lungs (to check if you are doing this correctly *see pages 29–30*).

You shouldn't worry if you can't see immediate results when you start using this witnessing technique or the Counting Backward breathing exercise above. Remember that your emotional well-being is a continual process of growth, breath by breath.

DIRECTING PRANA

"Prana is force on every plane of being, from the highest to the lowest. Whatever moves or works or has life is but an expression or manifestation of prana."

Swami Sivananda, Bliss Divine (1887–1963)

You may not be aware of it, but you receive prana all the time – from the food you eat, the water you drink, from sunlight and the air you breathe, and from the people around you. You also give it away to others. Usually this is an unconscious exchange of energy. If you feel unwell and a friend places her hand on your forehead, she is transferring her prana to you through her compassion. If you stumble and instinctively hold your breath and take both hands to your injured knee, you are directing an increased flow of prana to the area to speed healing. A yoga teacher who asks you to breathe into your hips is suggesting that you re-direct prana to that region to invigorate your pose.

If your body is healthy and full of vitality, you naturally affect those around you in a positive way when you transfer your prana, consciously or unconsciously. People enjoy being with you because they feel invigorated by the encounter. But when you feel distressed or lacking in positive energy, others may find your presence emotionally draining.

By practising the breathing visualization opposite, you can start to channel your prana consciously in order to become that vital, positive person that people want to engage with.

If you would like to take this conscious command of prana further, you can learn to manipulate it to heal yourself and others. The healing process works by directing prana to areas of

VISUALIZATION TO INCREASE PRANA FLOW

This exercise helps to recharge you and can lift your mood whenever you feel "down" – when you are charged with prana, you are more likely to be able to transfer your energy positively to others. This is also an effective way to top up your prana before using energy-healing techniques.

1 Gently sealing your lips, slowly breathe in through your nose to a mental count of 8 and then exhale through your nose to a count of 8.

2 Now breathe in again through your nose to a count of 8, but this time visualize prana streaming into you, intermingled with the air you inhale. You might like to visualize the prana as a current of bright light.

3 Hold your breath for a count of 4 and in your mind's eye picture the prana circulating through every part of your body.

4 Exhale through your mouth to a count of 8, feeling negativity leaving your body with the stale air. Repeat for as many breaths as you like.

your body that need help and by breaking up blockages in energy channels to allow prana to flow unimpeded (*see pages 23–4*). A good flow of prana stimulates cells and tissues and encourages the elimination of toxins, helping to restore healthy activity to that part of your body.

If this type of healing appeals to you, then why not investigate workshops or courses in one of the many popular techniques that work by transferring prana? These include reiki, Pranic Healing and Therapeutic Touch. Practitioners of these techniques may place their hands on or near a recipient, tune into their prana, focus their intention, and then allow the vitalizing energy to flow through their hands and into the receiver. Other practitioners believe that their prana is drawn out by the recipient's injury in order to activate or enhance the body's natural healing processes.

LETTING GO

Your world and your character are moulded by your thoughts. If you look for beauty everywhere, your life will seem joyous. But if you continually tell yourself that you are weak, you will find that you do indeed lack strength; while if you tend to focus on grief and loss, those experiences could become an integral part of your personality. The ancient yoga texts teach us that the more you hold onto or engage with negativity, the more that negativity will control you.

Prana breathing exercises can help you to create healing and empowering mental images that rejuvenate your mind, so that the prana you inhale encourages new and inspiring ways of being to emerge. It is as easy as picturing yourself inhaling prana with each in-breath, and imagining yourself letting go of destructive thinking on your out-breath. By accentuating the exhalation you encourage mental rejuvenation – just as when you exhale fully you allow a new in-breath of fresh, oxygen-rich air to effortlessly rush into your lungs.

But it can be very difficult to let go of negative thinking and be more positive. We might compare it to the difficulty, on a physical level, of exhaling fully. Even if you are able to breathe in deeply, you may not have the strength to fully release the stale air from your body – it actually takes more muscle power and physical strength to push the air out of your lungs than it does to breathe in. If you exhale only partially, on the next in-breath you will inhale that oxygen-depleted air again, which not only leaves your body deprived of the oxygen it needs, but cheats your emotions out of a fully vitalizing dose of prana. The 2:1 Breathing exercise opposite will help you whether you find it difficult to exhale fully or you have a tendency to dwell on negative thoughts. It aims to strengthen your powers of exhalation to help you to rid yourself of toxins and negative thinking and leaves your mind ready to be filled with positive thoughts.

2:1 BREATHING

This exercise helps you to develop a long, full exhalation. This stimulates your parasympathetic nervous system, which helps you to let go of mental stressors, physical tension and negative emotions. Use it as a preparation for meditation or whenever you feel overwhelmed by negativity and crave an injection of inspiring, positive prana. Start by sitting comfortably, preferably with your legs crossed (*see pages 35–7*).

1 Sit with your back straight and gently seal your lips. Start to notice whether you are taking full breaths in and out through your nose using every part of your lungs (*see pages 28–30*). Your breath should be smooth and soundless, and there should be no pause between the inhalation and exhalation.

2 If you are new to breathing exercises, begin by exhaling for 6 seconds and inhaling for just 3 seconds. If you find this too difficult, lessen your exhalation to 4 seconds and inhale for 2 seconds.

3 To enhance the release of difficult emotions, mentally repeat the word "let" with each inhalation. On each exhalation, silently say the word "go".

4 Keep breathing and repeating the words. With each long exhalation visualize stress and anxiety leaving your system along with the stale air in your lungs. Say goodbye to long-held muscle tension and let go of self-imposed mental boundaries or emotional limitations, releasing whatever is holding you back in life. Continue for 1–3 minutes, then gently stretch before getting up.

ALIGNING YOUR ENERGIES

"The sun (right nostril) and the moon (left nostril) divide time into day and night."
Hatha Yoga Pradipika, 4.17

The left side of your brain controls the right side of your body, while the right side of your brain governs the left side of your body. Yoga philosophy teaches that your breathing is closely connected with the natural shifts in function between these two sides of your brain as they work together to operate your body. It is affected by the flow of prana through your two main energy channels, the ida (left) and pingala (right) nadis (*see page 23*), which are thought to equate with your left and right nostrils.

To experience the effect these channels have on your physical body, hold the back of your hand beneath one nostril. Breathe out through your nose. Then move the back of your hand beneath the other nostril and breathe out again. You will notice that your breath is stronger on one side then the other. If you repeat this experiment a couple of hours later, you may find that your breath is stronger on the other side. In a healthy person without a cold or other respiratory blockage, your dominant breath will probably change sides every 1½ to 2 hours. From an energetic point of view, this is explained as a normal change in predominance of the energy in your ida or pingala channels.

Breathing through your right nostril stimulates prana, your energizing breath, while breathing through your left nostril stimulates apana, your calming and releasing breath (*see chapter 5, pages 104–127*). The top exercise opposite helps you to experience that shift from vitalizing to calming energy, and can be of help both at busy times of day, when you need to raise your energy, and at night to calm you before bed. The bottom exercise prepares you for full Alternate Nostril Breathing (*see page 55*), which promotes equilibrium between the two energies and brings you into a state of meditation. Practise both exercises equally.

SINGLE NOSTRIL BREATHING

Practise step 1 in the morning and step 2 in the evening, sitting comfortably, preferably with your legs crossed (*see pages 35–7*).

1 In the morning: sit with your back straight and gently seal your lips. Rest your left hand on your left thigh and position your right hand in Vishnu Mudra (*see page 54*), palm in front of your face. Close your left nostril with your right ring and little fingers. Inhale deeply through your right nostril for a count of 4 and exhale for a count of 8. Repeat 10 times and then relax.

2 In the evening: repeat, but closing your right nostril using your right thumb. Inhale through your left nostril for a count of 4 and exhale for a count of 8. Repeat 10 times, using all your lung capacity (*see page 29*), and then relax.

SIMPLE ALTERNATE NOSTRIL BREATHING

This is best practised at noon, before lunch, sitting with your legs crossed (*see pages 35–7*). After mastering this exercise, progress to page 55.

1 Sit with your back straight and gently seal your lips. Rest your left hand on your left thigh, palm facing upward and position your right hand in Vishnu Mudra (*see page 54*), holding your palm in front of your face.

2 Close your right nostril with your right thumb and inhale through your left nostril for a count of 4. Close your left nostril with your ring–little fingers.

3 Lift your thumb and exhale through your right nostril for a count of 8. Then inhale through the same nostril for a count of 4.

4 Close your right nostril with your thumb and lift your fingers to exhale through your left nostril to a count of 8. Repeat 10 times, using every part of your lungs (*see page 29*) before relaxing.

INTEGRATING YOUR COMPLEMENTARY HALVES

"The sun is the prana of the universe. It rises to help the prana in the eye to see."
Prasna Upanishad, 3.8

Yoga philosophy regards the right side of your body (and left side of the brain) as the seat of masculine qualities. It is considered rational, warm and outwardly directed, and is represented in the yogic tradition by the god Siva and in the Chinese tradition by the yang part of the yin-yang symbol. The left side of your body (and the right side of the brain) is considered the seat of feminine qualities — intuitive, cool and inwardly directed — and is represented by the goddess Shakti and yin. In the yin-yang symbol, each half has its opposing quality contained within it, just as each of us has both masculine and feminine characteristics. If these fall out of balance, your prana diminishes and your well-being suffers. Restoring balance involves reintegrating the intuitive with the rational, and the feminine with the masculine. You can do this by practising the Alternate Nostril Breathing exercise, opposite. It equalizes the flow of breath through your left and right energy channels, allowing prana energy to vitalize your body and mind, and apana energy (*see page 104*) to calm your emotions, release stress and prepare you for meditation. With regular practice, you may notice that you feel more "grounded".

VISHNU MUDRA

This mudra, or yogic hand position, enables you to seal the energy of your breath inside your body. Raise your right hand (even if you are left-handed) and bend your index and middle fingers into the palm of your hand (see left). This leaves your thumb free to close your right nostril and your ring and little fingers free to close your left nostril.

ALTERNATE NOSTRIL BREATHING
ANULOMA VILOMA

Try this exercise once you are comfortable with the simpler version on page 53. If you find it difficult to hold your breath for a count of 16, hold it for 8 and gradually increase it. Keep the other counts in proportion – for every second you inhale, retain your breath for four times as long and exhale for twice as long. Start by sitting comfortably (*see pages 35–7*).

1 Sit with your back straight and gently seal your lips. Position your right hand in Vishnu Mudra (*see opposite, below*) in front of your face. Rest your left hand on your left knee, palm facing upward.

2 Exhale fully, then close your right nostril with your thumb. Inhale through your left nostril for a count of 4 (*see image* A).

A

3 Gently pinch both nostrils shut between your thumb, and ring and little fingers. Hold your breath for a count of 16 – four times as long as your inhalation (*see image* B).

4 Release your thumb from your right nostril, keeping your left nostril closed with your ring and little fingers. Breathe out through your right nostril for a count of 8 – twice the count of the inhalation (*see image* C).

B

5 Keeping your left nostril closed, breathe in through your right nostril for a count of 4. Then, pinch both nostrils shut and hold your breath for a count of 16.

6 Release your left nostril, keeping the right nostril closed with your thumb. Breathe out through the left nostril for a count of 8. This is one round. Gradually build up to 10 rounds daily. You may increase the count, but keep to the ratio 1–4–2.

C

CAUTION: AVOID IF YOU ARE PREGNANT: INSTEAD PRACTISE
SIMPLE ALTERNATE NOSTRIL BREATHING ON PAGE 53.

BREATHING FOR BALANCE

"Life is prana, prana is life. So long as prana remains in this body, so long is there life. Through prana, one obtains, even in this world, immortality."
Kaushitaki Upanishad, 3.2

If you tune into your energy patterns as they shift between your right and left energy channels every couple of hours throughout the day (*see page 52*), you may find that you can synchronize your breathing with the relevant hemisphere of your brain. When practised regularly, this can bring about profound changes in your levels of vitalizing prana energy and positivity, giving you the ability to function at optimal capacity throughout the day. Start by learning which nostril to breathe through to affect particular activities (*see box, opposite*). If your current activity does not correspond to the nostril with the more forceful flow of breath at that moment (check by briefly holding the back of your hand beneath your nostrils), change the flow of energy by gently pressing the more open nostril closed. Try to breathe through your more congested nostril if you can. This becomes easier if you practise breathing exercises regularly.

As a rule, times when the rational, analytical and mathematical left hemisphere of your brain (your right energy channel) is dominant are good for sequential, linear and logical tasks and information processing,

SWARA YOGA

The Sanskrit word swara *can be translated as "the sound of your own breath". An esoteric branch of yoga known as swara yoga teaches ways of analyzing your breath and tuning into the different pranic rhythms and the subtle bio-rhythms of your body and mind. It encourages you to synchronize the activities of your daily life with your breath. If you would like to find out more, turn to the further reading recommendations on page 157.*

such as doing accounts, memorizing a script or planning a party. You will complete these tasks most efficiently if you breathe predominately through your right nostril. Conversely, creative or artistic endeavours and tasks that involve your orientation in space, such as dancing or map-reading, will be more fruitful when your intuitive and holistic right hemisphere (your left energy channel) is dominant. Enhance this energy by breathing through your left nostril. Ancient yoga texts state that on the few occasions that the breath flows evenly through both nostrils, your awareness extends beyond time and space. This is a time for spiritual activities, such as meditation, prayer and expressions of compassion. Alternate Nostril Breathing (*see page 55*) can bring you into this balanced state.

LEFT NOSTRIL/ RIGHT BRAIN ACTIVITIES	RIGHT NOSTRIL/ LEFT BRAIN ACTIVITIES
Associative thinking	Mathematical reasoning
Creative, calm, silent work	Physical activities
Drinking water	Eating
Leaving home	Returning home
Re-arranging furniture	Doing accounts
Working with shapes or forms	Working with words and numbers
Non-verbal communication	Speaking and debating
Singing, playing, composing or listening to music	Reading, writing, studying or listening to words

PRANA EXERCISE SEQUENCE:

SALUTING THE SUN

Yoga teachers will tell you that while the air you inhale travels directly into your lungs, the prana you take in with it moves along your spine. The flowing routine demonstrated over the following pages enhances your intake of vitalizing energy because each of its poses is intimately connected with your breathing and the sequence extends your spine forward and back. As you enjoy the dance-like movements, feel the increased intake of prana vitalizing your body and mind. When practised early in the morning, the Sun Salutation helps to regulate your breath for the rest of the day. Begin by doing six Sun Salutations daily (three on each side) and gradually increase your practice to 12 rounds, leading the first round with your right foot, the second with your left, and so on.

SUN SALUTATION

If you are a complete beginner and find that there is just too much to remember in this sequence, ignore the breathing instructions to begin with and simply learn the body positions. Once you are more familiar with the sequence, begin to co-ordinate your movements with your in- and out-breaths in order to maximize your intake of vitalizing prana.

CAUTION: IF YOU ARE PREGNANT, MODIFY THE MOVES – DO NOT LIFT YOUR ARMS OVER YOUR HEAD NOR REST YOUR ABDOMEN ON THE GROUND. IT IS BEST TO LEARN WITH A TEACHER WHO SPECIALIZES IN PREGNANCY YOGA.

1   Begin by standing tall with your feet together and your arms relaxed by your sides. Gently seal your mouth and inhale deeply through your nose, preparing yourself mentally to begin the sequence of movements. Remember to breathe through your nose throughout the sequence.

2   Breathe out as you bring your palms together directly in front of your breastbone in the prayer position of classical yoga. Feel this movement begin to "centre" both your body and your mind.

3   Breathe in as you straighten your elbows and stretch your arms overhead. Try to keep your arms straight and beside your ears as you look up. Simultaneously arch your entire body backward, trying to keep your knees and elbows straight. Feel this complete stretch energizing your whole body, from your fingers to your toes.

4   Exhale as you bend forward to place your hands on the ground at either side of your feet. If you are unable to reach the ground with your knees straight, bend your knees slightly. Try to bring your forehead toward your knees.

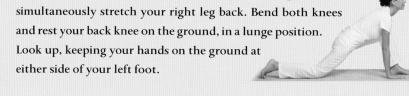

5 Inhale deeply to take in as much prana as possible and simultaneously stretch your right leg back. Bend both knees and rest your back knee on the ground, in a lunge position. Look up, keeping your hands on the ground at either side of your left foot.

6 Retain your breath as you bring your left foot back in line with your right foot. Straighten both knees to bring your body into a push-up position, forming a straight line with your body from your head to your heels, if you can.

7 Exhale as you bend your knees and place them on the ground. Keep your hips up and place your chest on the ground between your hands. Bring your chin to the ground.

8 Without moving your hands or your feet, inhale and slide your body forward, then arch up your head and chest. Keep your hands flat on the ground and your elbows slightly bent, tucking them in toward your sides. Relax your shoulders down, away from your ears. Make sure you keep your lower body on the ground.

9 Tuck your toes under and breathe out as you lift your hips as high as possible. Try not to move your hands or feet. Straighten your elbows and allow your head to hang down between your arms. Bring your chest closer to your thighs as you stretch your heels toward the ground. This is Downward Dog pose and can be practised on its own, too.

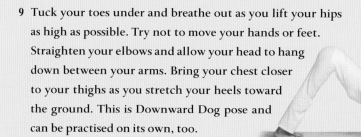

10 Inhale, bend your left knee and rest it on the ground. Almost simultaneously, step forward with your right foot, bringing the toes in line with your fingers. Look up without lifting your hands off the ground.

11 Exhaling, bring your left foot forward, positioning it beside your right. Lift your hips up and drop your head toward your knees. Straighten your knees as much as possible without lifting your hands off the ground. Remember that you can bend your knees slightly, if you need to.

12 Inhale as you slowly straighten your body and stand upright. Stretch your arms forward and then up over your head. Try to keep your arms straight and beside your ears. Look up. Simultaneously arch your entire body backward, trying to keep your knees and elbows straight. Again, feel this whole-body stretch energizing you from your fingers to your toes.

13 Exhale as you lower your arms by your sides and return to your starting position. This completes one round of the Sun Salutation sequence. In the next round, stretch your left leg back in step 5 and step forward with your left foot in step 10.

CHAPTER 3

YOUR NOURISHING BREATH

UNDERSTANDING SAMANA

Most people think of breathing as the process of taking air into the lungs and letting it out again, but these are only the first and final stages of the process. After prana, your vitalizing breath, has filled your lungs with air, the second of the five forms of subtle energy flowing through your body, samana, begins its work – extracting oxygen to transport to your cells. This is similar to the work your digestive system does when it breaks down food into its constituent nutrients. Indeed, yoga philosophers say that samana ("centring" or "balancing" energy) nourishes your body by controlling both gaseous exchange in your lungs and the digestive process in your stomach.

The region of the body most affected by samana energy

In the following pages, you will find out how samana also feeds your mind by helping you to digest ideas, interpret feelings and make sense of arguments. By boosting your samana energy using the breathing exercises in this chapter, you not only maximize the oxygen and nutrients in your system, you transform the way you engage with ideas and feelings to nourish your intellectual and emotional life, too.

YOUR DIGESTING BREATH

If you imagine, once again, that your body is a factory, samana would be the department in charge of processing the raw materials ordered in by the boss: prana (*see pages 40–41*). Samana extracts all the substances you can use – oxygen from the air you inhale, nutrients from your food, and ideas from the words and sounds you are exposed to – and passes them on to the relevant processing place, ready to be absorbed into your bloodstream or your thought processes. Samana then permits apana, your cleansing breath, to release what you no longer need (*see pages 106–7*). Within your body, the strongest influence of this nourishing breath is around your solar plexus, which extends from the bottom of your ribcage down to your navel.

Samana is the energy of moderation, and you can best support it by following a path of moderation in your daily life – by eating a balanced diet, taking some exercise every day, getting enough sleep and trying to keep your emotions on an even keel – as well as by practising specific breathing exercises. Because samana is a heating energy, when it falls out of balance it can overheat your system physically or emotionally. The breathing exercises on the following pages demonstrate effective ways to diffuse this excess heat. For example, if you notice your emotions heating up, take a few deep breaths, then try the Cooling Breath or Hissing Breath on page 77. If you often become emotionally overheated, you can cool your samana energy by replacing caffeinated drinks with chamomile tea, and by avoiding spicy food, onions and garlic.

If, conversely, your samana energy is sapped or dampened down – signs may include digestive symptoms or finding yourself withdrawing from arguments and avoiding issues – this chapter is also for you. Exercises such as Sun Breathing (*see page 71*), Bellows Breath (*see page 75*) and Fire Purification (*see page 73*) will help to revive the inner fire you lack, re-engage your mind with the world, and encourage you to deal

WORKING WITH SAMANA ENERGY

As you use the breathing exercises in this chapter, ask yourself these questions. They can help you to see how you are over-heating or depleting your samana and find ways in which you could rebalance it.

- *Do I have digestive problems?*
- *Am I often angry? If so, do I express my anger in a healthy way?*
- *Do I often bury negative experiences and thoughts? How might I start to confront and deal with them instead?*
- *Do I continually mull over everything that happens to me? How can I stop myself from getting lost in daydreams?*
- *Am I inclined to say that things are OK when I know that they aren't, to avoid a "scene"?*
- *Do I tend to repeat what I hear verbatim. Or do I think things through and then decide for myself?*
- *Am I a hoarder? Or do I let go of possessions I no longer love or need?*
- *Do I manage my money wisely?*
- *How important is it for me to be surrounded by beautiful things? Can I make more time to nurture myself in this way?*

with issues rather than withdraw from them. You may feel more "fired up" with samana energy if you also refrain from iced drinks and wait at least 30 minutes after a meal before drinking anything at all. Try not to overeat or take your main meal late in the evening, and avoid heavy, oily or very cold foods, too.

When your samana energy is strong yet well balanced, you will feel better nourished with oxygen and nutrients. The fire in your belly will help you to assimilate negative experiences and remain detached from energy-draining situations, and your more focused concentration will equip you with the equilibrium to be able to make discerning decisions about what you want from life.

SAMANA VISUALIZATION:
CONCENTRATING YOUR SAMANA

Samana draws energy inward from your peripheries and concentrates it around the centre of your body, storing excess safely in your body's energetic battery, around your solar plexus. From this control centre, samana governs your body's ability to digest food and oxygen, sensory experiences and intellectual stimulation. This is also the site of your manipura chakra (*see page 25*), the subtle energy centre related to your willpower and self-esteem. Here is the meeting point where your in-breath changes form to become your out-breath. You might like to visualize it as an energetic junction where you switch from one state to another – from the inward-moving energy of prana (your vitalizing breath, *see chapter 2*) to the outward-expanding energy of apana (your cleansing breath, *see chapter 5*).

Modern life seems to be characterized by an excessive flow of energy outward. Your mind, senses and bank balances are constantly over-stimulated. This can leave you feeling depleted of energy. If your samana energy is too weak, you may feel greedy for new sensations, over-emotional or "stuck" in some way. Use the Samana Breathing exercise opposite to help contain and concentrate your energy when it is being depleted by external demands, so that you feel more in charge and better balanced. To nourish your samana energy further, visualize the exchange of oxygen and waste in your lungs as you retain your breath.

HARNESSING SAMANA

Have you ever woken in the morning bemused by a dream? When you ponder the meaning of a dream in this way, you call on the power of your samana energy, which encourages your intellect to "pull things together". To stimulate this energy further, focus on contracting movements when you exercise, such as bending forward, or relax with a jigsaw puzzle.

SAMANA BREATHING EXERCISE

Start by sitting comfortably, preferably with your legs crossed (*see pages 35–7*). This exercise is best practised outdoors, but if this is not possible, contemplate a picture of a landscape. Before you begin, take in the view. Let your inner essence be fed by the colours of the plants, trees and sky.

1 Sit with your back straight and gently seal your lips. Close your eyes and inhale deeply through your nose, drawing your breath into your belly.

2 At the end of your inhalation, hold your breath, keeping your focus firmly on your solar plexus. Visualize your samana energy here as a multi-coloured, multi-dimensional stream of energy spiralling inward. Feel how it provides your body with stability and a sense of equilibrium.

3 Exhale slowly through your nose, feeling samana energy centring every part of your being. Visualize an infinite well of energy around your solar plexus from which you can withdraw nourishment for your body, mind and spirit whenever you feel the need. Repeat 3–5 times, then open your eyes.

SAMANA FABLE:
A BALANCE OF ENERGIES

"Once upon a time, two birds were sitting together, one on each side of a strong wooden perch. Although they shared this living space, the birds never looked at one another. Sometimes one bird would move toward the other, but this unbalanced the perch, and so he would instinctively move away again to bring their shared space back into balance. Once in a while, one of the birds would try to fly away. However, he would only be able to fly a short distance before being drawn back to the perch by a length of vine tethered to his foot. Although there was no possibility of getting away from the perch, neither bird understood why. The two birds lived together without knowing that they were tied both to the perch and to the actions of their partner."

Interpreting the tale

Imagine that prana — your inward-moving, vitalizing energy — is one of these birds who share the perch. Imagine that the other bird is apana, your outward-pushing, cleansing energy. Both need to be in equilibrium to keep you well-balanced in mind and body. During the process of breathing, prana equates with your in-breath and apana with your out-breath. Samana energy is the pause between them — a retention of breath also referred

HERBS TO BALANCE YOUR BREATHING

These herbs may be recommended to support the respiratory system by practitioners of Ayurveda or Traditional Chinese Medicine. Though you can buy the herbs in health-food stores and online, it's best to be diagnosed and have doses prescribed by a qualified herbalist.

GINSENG is a restorative tonic for the lungs and adrenals, and can help to strengthen your lungs when they have been weakened by chronic colds or a cough and/or general exhaustion.

BALA, a popular Ayurvedic herb, is prescribed as a tonic and restorative for the respiratory, cardiovascular and nervous systems.

TULSI, India's holy basil, is recommended in the Ayurvedic healthcare system to cleanse the lungs. It has antioxidant and anti-fungal properties, and encourages your body's innate ability to deal with stress.

CITRUS PEEL, a Chinese herb used to cleanse the lungs of excessive mucus, harmonizes and warms the digestion, reducing mucus.

to as your "middle breath", whose role is to unite your prana and apana. It is your samana energy that balances both birds on the perch so that their movements become complementary rather than opposing, and permits each bird a measure of freedom, while ensuring that they always return to each other to maintain homeostasis.

One of the most effective ways of improving the relationship between your prana and your apana energies is by increasing your samana — the breath-retention between your in- and out-breaths. Ancient yogis devised breathing exercises to increase the length of this retention, and you might like to begin exploring this by practising the Sun Breathing technique on page 71. Holding your breath has the added benefit of purifying your subtle energy, increasing your ability to assimilate — or digest — mental, emotional and spiritual stimuli, and to store excess energy around your solar plexus, providing the reserves you need to make discriminating choices about your future.

DRAWING ON THE WARMTH OF THE SUN

"Through mastery of the mid-breath which nourishes your body [samana],
you shine with a radiant light."
Yoga Sutra, 3.40

The Sun Breathing exercise opposite is one of the best ways of enhancing your samana. By inhaling through your right nostril, the pingala energy channel associated with the sun (*see page 23*), you increase your body heat, stimulate your digestion and switch on your sympathetic nervous system to ease symptoms of stress. Sun Breathing is especially beneficial if you suffer from problems arising from a lack of body heat. In yogic thought, this includes colds and congestion, obesity, oedema, muscle stiffness, sleepiness, lethargy, mental dullness, fatigue and depression. But this practice stimulates more than physical warmth – by promoting samana, it also enhances dynamism and emotional sensitivity, which can help you to feel more extroverted. You may therefore find Sun Breathing helpful if you have difficulty in communicating or expressing your creativity.

Invigorating Sun Breathing is best practised as a morning wake-up exercise or as a tonic for the 3pm "blues". As it stimulates your mind, it is best not to practise it in the evening if you have trouble falling asleep.

BREATHING AND NUTRITION

When tired or stressed, it is tempting to reach for a quick energy fix, such as fast food, caffeinated drinks, alcohol or tobacco. While these provide instant energy, they tire your body in the long run. For a constant, more holistic flow of energy, practise Sun Breathing (see opposite) and Fire Purification (see page 73), which enhance your metabolism and raise your digestive fire, converting food to a more readily usable form. However, do remember that breathing exercises are no substitute for a nutritious and moderate diet.

SUN BREATHING

SURYA BHEDA

Inhaling through your right nostril heats your body, while exhaling through your left nostril releases excess energy and impurities. Sit comfortably, preferably with your legs crossed (*see pages 35–7*). Practise on an empty stomach. Do not worry if you feel perspiration at the roots of your hair as you retain your breath – this is a healthy sign.

1 Sit with your back straight and gently seal your lips. Position your right hand in Vishnu Mudra (*see page 54*), with your palm in front of your face.

2 Close your left nostril with the little and ring fingers of your right hand. Silently inhale deeply through your right nostril.

3 Pinch both nostrils shut by closing your right nostril with your right thumb. Hold your breath for as long as you feel comfortable.

4 Release the pressure on your left nostril and exhale very slowly without making any sound. Repeat 10 times a day, always inhaling through your right nostril and exhaling through your left, and then relax. Gradually increase your daily practice to 20 repetitions.

CAUTION: AVOID IF YOU SUFFER FROM HIGH BLOOD PRESSURE, FEVER, SKIN RASHES, ANOREXIA, ATTENTION DEFICIT DISORDER, INSOMNIA, RESTLESSNESS AND/OR NERVOUS AGITATION.

FIRING UP POSITIVE ENERGY

Samana energy is concentrated around your solar plexus region. This is the home of your digestive fire, known in the yogic tradition as *agni*. The traditional medicine of India, Ayurveda, views agni as the foundation of good health. When, this inner fire is strong, you digest your food well, absorb plentiful vital energy from the air you breathe and enjoy a congenial relationship with the world around you. Conversely, weak agni is thought to contribute to and aggravate many chronic health conditions – including both physical illnesses and psychological imbalances.

The Fire Purification exercise given here (*see opposite, below*) is an important yogic breathing technique used to stimulate and awaken both your digestive fire and the energy of samana, your nourishing breath. With regular practice, it increases the vitality and robustness of your entire abdominal region. This, in turn, has a positive effect on the whole of your energy system, the clarity of your thinking and your ability to focus your attention effectively. It can also counteract sagging abdominal muscles and relieve constipation.

Fire Purification is quite an intense exercise, so prepare for it by first mastering the Abdominal Lift (*see opposite, above*), a powerful exercise in its own right. The Sanskrit name (*uddiyana*) indicates that this exercise strengthens not only your samana energy, but also acts with your expressive breath (udana; *see chapter 6*) to enhance your will-power and enjoyment of life. When you first begin to practise this lift you may become re-acquainted with abdominal muscles you have not consciously used for years. Most people find it easiest to do this exercise standing, but as an alternative, you may also sit with your legs crossed (*see pages 35–7*).

ABDOMINAL LIFT
UDDIYANA

Try to practise on an empty stomach, preferably first thing in the morning. When you have mastered this, progress to the exercise below.

1 Stand with feet hip-width apart and knees slightly bent. Try not to turn out your toes. Lean forward, resting your hands on your thighs, fingers facing in.

2 Take a deep breath in through your nose, then forcefully exhale through your mouth, trying to push all the air out of your lungs. Simultaneously straighten your elbows, tuck your tailbone forward slightly and lower your chin toward your chest – imagine there is a string pulling your diaphragm up toward your throat.

3 Hold the pose for as long as you can comfortably keep your breath out. Then release your abdomen and inhale deeply. Rest briefly, then repeat 3–5 times.

FIRE PURIFICATION
AGNI SARA

Begin by practising the Abdominal Lift (see above), again making sure that you practise on an empty stomach.

1 When you reach the holding position (at the end of step 2), do not breathe in, but release your diaphragm and quickly contract it again.

2 Repeat the release and contraction 5–10 times – or for as long as you can hold your breath out. When necessary, take an in-breath, and then rest briefly before repeating. Repeat 1–2 times daily, building up to several times a day.

CAUTION: DO NOT PRACTISE EITHER OF THESE EXERCISES IF YOU HAVE HIGH BLOOD PRESSURE OR CARDIOVASCULAR DISEASE, OR ARE PREGNANT OR MENSTRUATING.

IGNITING MOTIVATION

*"Draw in the breath and exhale it as directed. Go on, again and again,
as the blacksmith works his bellows rapidly."*
Hatha Yoga Pradipika, 2.62

One of the most powerful of yogic breathing exercises, Bellows Breath (*see opposite*) is a useful way to strengthen your samana energy while stoking your digestive fire and "firing" you up with inspiration. It also clears your sinuses and lungs, massages your organs of digestion, and gives your cardiovascular system a workout. As you practise, feel how it forces you to use all your chest and abdominal muscles, first to strongly pull air into your lungs and then to expel it with equal vigour. (Compare this to the relatively gentle cleansing of the effortless inhalation in the Purifying Breath exercise on page 32.) It is these powerful, rapid and extremely active inhalations and exhalations that stimulate your motivation. The intense movements of your lungs and ribcage in and out – like a blacksmith's bellows – also give the exercise its name. Bellows Breath generates so much heat in your body that many yoga traditions refer to it as the Breath of Fire. For this reason, do not over-heat your body by practising in the summer or when the sun is high. It's best done in the early morning. If you're a beginner, first spend some time mastering Purifying Breath (*see page 32*) and Fire Purification (*see page 73*). However, be aware that Bellows Breath, like all advanced breathing exercises, is best learned from a qualified yoga teacher.

BELLOWS BREATH
BHASTRIKA

Start by sitting with your legs crossed or kneeling (*see pages 35–7*) and take 3–4 full, deep breaths, expanding your ribcage completely on each inhalation and keeping your spine straight (slumping impedes the intercostal muscles around the ribcage). Try not to reverse the action – pulling in your abdomen as you inhale can strain your nervous system.

1 Sit with your spine straight, your shoulders relaxed and lips gently sealed. Inhale deeply through your nose, then exhale quickly through your nose, forcefully pushing all the air out of your lungs.

2 Inhale again strongly, separating your ribs as far as possible to pull maximum air into your lungs. Try not to use your shoulders or allow your chest to drop, and keep your face relaxed.

3 Repeat the quick exhalation and strong inhalation in rapid succession. Contract your lungs, ribcage and abdomen to the maximum with each exhalation and expand them as far as possible with each inhalation.

4 Keep your in- and out-breaths equal in strength and listen to the breath as it moves in and out of your lungs – your inhalations and exhalations should be equally loud. If you feel light-headed or get a "stitch" in your side, stop and take a few deep breaths to relax your respiratory system.

5 At first, do fewer repetitions of very vigorous breaths – try to take one full breath (inhalation and exhalation) every second. Do this 5–7 times, then breathe normally for a minute or so. Do 2 rounds per sitting, then relax. Gradually increase your rate to 2 breaths per second, with 15–20 breaths per round. It is best to limit yourself to 3 or fewer rounds per sitting.

CAUTION: DO NOT PRACTISE IF YOU ARE MENSTRUATING OR PREGNANT, OR IF YOUR NOSE IS BLOCKED. AVOID IF YOU SUFFER FROM HEART DISEASE OR HIGH BLOOD PRESSURE. IF YOU HAVE ASTHMA, PRACTISE THE PURIFYING BREATH INSTEAD (*SEE PAGE 32*).

COOLING YOUR ANGER

"This pranayama called sheetali destroys diseases of the abdomen and spleen, also fever, bilious complaints, hunger, thirst and the negative effects of poisons, such as snakebites."
Hatha Yoga Pradipika, 2.57–58

If you have a need always to excel and are very ambitious, or frequently feel irritable or angry, then your samana energy may be too strong, causing you to "heat up". If so, you would benefit from energy-cooling practices, such as the breathing exercises opposite, which can help to cool you down emotionally as well as physically.

The Sanskrit name for the Cooling Breath, *sheetali*, can be translated as "calm", "passionless" or "unemotional", and this indicates its effect on fiery conditions of the mind and emotions. Yoga teachers recommend this exercise to "cool down" chronic physical problems arising from excessive heat in the body, such as fevers, skin rashes, stomach ulcers, hyperacidity and even bee stings.

If you are unable to master the tongue-rolling of the Cooling Breath opposite, above (some people find it anatomically impossible), then try the Hissing Breath, opposite, below, which replicates many of its cooling effects. While cooling the temperature of a heated mind and emotions, this practice is also said to enhance the beauty and vigour of your body.

TENSION TIP

Although stressful reactions such as anger may be an unavoidable fact of life, don't allow them to drain your energy. Next time you feel yourself "heating up" — your blood pressure rising, heart starting to pump faster or sweat prickling your skin — stop for a moment and try one of the cooling exercises opposite. While calming body and emotions, they bring in extra brain-nourishing oxygen so you can work out how best to deal with a difficult situation.

COOLING BREATH
SHEETALI

This is especially good for quelling anger and cooling your system in summer, the best season to practise (ideally, at midday). Start by sitting comfortably (*see pages 35–7*).

A

1 Sit with your back straight. Stick your tongue out a little way past your lips. Try to roll the sides of your tongue upward and together to form a tube (*see image* A). If you find this difficult, then don't worry – try the Hissing Breath instead (*see below*).

2 Draw air into your mouth through your tongue-tube, as if you are drinking it through a straw.

3 Hold your breath for as long as you feel comfortable, then exhale through both nostrils. Repeat 3–5 times and then relax.

HISSING BREATH
SITKARI

This exercise counteracts extreme heat by cooling your system. It also helps to develop a single-minded focus. As with the exercise above, try not to practise in cold weather.

B

1 Sit as before with your back straight (*see above*). Open your mouth a little, then fold your tongue back so that the tip touches the hard ridge behind your teeth (*see image* B).

2 Try to bring your teeth back together and inhale by drawing air in through your mouth, making a hissing sound.

3 Immediately exhale slowly through both nostrils. Repeat the exercise 2–5 times and then relax.

SAMANA EXERCISE SEQUENCE:
FIVE RITES OF REJUVENATION

Also known as the Five Tibetan Rites, or more simply as the "Tibetans", this series of exercises is reputed to nourish and regenerate your body and mind, thus strengthening your samana energy. The best time to practise them is in the early morning, and as you practise, keep directing your thoughts to the seat of your nourishing samana breath in your solar plexus region, where your body's digestive fire has its spark. The whole sequence is quite demanding, but even if you do find some of the exercises challenging at first, be sure to do at least one of each, gradually building up to the optimum number – 21.

TIBETAN EXERCISE SEQUENCE

This sequence consists of five exercises, each of which are repeated several times, plus an "interim breath" to settle you between each one. Start by practising 3–4 repetitions of each exercise, gradually building up to 21 (it is best not to exceed this amount). Eventually you should be able to complete them all in 5–6 minutes. Before you begin the sequence, stand for a moment with your eyes closed. Take a few deep breaths and imagine guiding the breath into your solar plexus, the site of your samana. When you feel ready, open your eyes and begin the sequence, but return to this static standing position if you feel dizzy or exhausted at any time.

CAUTION: AVOID IF YOU ARE PREGNANT, HAVE HIGH BLOOD PRESSURE OR ARE PRONE TO DIZZINESS. CONSULT A DOCTOR IF YOU HAVE CONCERNS OVER WHETHER THESE EXERCISES ARE SUITABLE FOR YOU.

FIRST TIBETAN RITE

1 Stand with your feet slightly apart. Stretch your arms straight out from your shoulders, keeping them parallel to the ground with your palms open and facing downward. Make sure that your fingers are straight and touching each other.

2 Look right and spin slowly clockwise, keeping your arms outstretched. At first, turn only 3–4 times, but as you gain in confidence, build up to 21 spins. With practise you will move beyond dizziness and experience your body as a whirlpool of energy with its centre at your solar plexus.

3 After spinning, stand with your feet hip-width apart with your hands on your hips, and then take an "interim breath" – breathe in fully through your nose, then round your lips and blow out the air through your mouth. Repeat 2–3 times, then practise the second rite.

SECOND TIBETAN RITE

1 Lie on your back with legs together, extending away from you. Rest your arms by your body, palms down. Flex your ankles, stretch your toes to your head and press the small of your back into the ground.

2 Inhaling, raise both legs together until the soles of your feet face the sky and the line of your legs is just over a right angle. Simultaneously, raise your head, bringing your chin toward your chest – try to make the leg and head lifts one smooth motion. Keep your lower back and buttocks on the floor.

3 Exhaling through your nose, lower your legs and head, using solar-plexus energy to keep your back flat. Without pausing, try to repeat the leg and head raises 3–4 times, building up to 21 repetitions. Stand up and take 2–3 interim breaths before practising the third rite.

THIRD TIBETAN RITE

1 Kneel with knees and feet slightly apart but parallel. Tuck your toes under, resting the balls of your feet on the ground. Place your hands on the backs of your thighs, just below your buttocks. Drop your chin to your chest.

2 Inhaling through your nose, arch back from your waist, dropping your head back. Lift your breastbone to the sky. Let your hands support your weight as your solar plexus stretches.

3 Exhaling, straighten up into your starting position with your chin on your chest. Without pausing, alternate between the back arch and head-forward position 3–4 times, building up to 21 repetitions. Stand up and take 2–3 interim breaths before practising the fourth rite.

FOURTH TIBETAN RITE

1 Sit with your legs stretched out. Place your palms beside your hips, fingers facing forward. Tuck your chin into your chest.

2 Inhaling through your nose, raise your hips, bend your knees and place the soles of your feet on the ground. Drop your head back if you can to make a "table-top", with your body parallel to the ground from head to knees. Think of your calves and arms as the table legs. Try not to let your feet slide.

3 Exhaling, drop your legs and buttocks, coming back to the starting position with your chin forward. Try not to bend your arms to achieve this, use your shoulders as a pivot point. Repeat, moving steadily between the table-top and sitting positions 3–4 times, building up to 21. Then stand up and take 2–3 interim breaths before practising the final rite.

FIFTH TIBETAN RITE

1 Lie on your front, with your legs hip-width apart. Place your palms beneath your shoulders with your fingers facing forward, and tuck your toes under, resting the balls of your feet on the ground. Straighten your arms until only your toes and hands are on the ground. Lift your head up and back. This is Upward Dog pose.

2 Exhaling through your nose, lift your hips toward the sky, drop your head and push back, keeping your arms straight. Press back with your chest. Push your hands and feet into the ground to distribute your weight evenly. This is Downward Dog pose (*see page 60*).

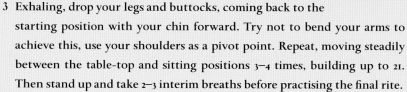

3 Inhaling, drop your hips to return to Upward Dog. Without pausing, switch between the poses 3–4 times, building up to 21. Then roll onto your back and relax, feeling your breath within your solar plexus.

CHAPTER 4

YOUR EXPANSIVE BREATH

UNDERSTANDING VYANA

After air has been brought into your body with an in-breath and its oxygen has filtered into your bloodstream, vyana, the third of the five forms of prana flowing through your body, begins its work. Vyana energy governs your circulatory system and makes sure that oxygen reaches every cell in your body. Without a constant supply of oxygen, metabolism cannot take place and the energy from your food cannot be made usable.

Ancient yoga texts tell us that vyana energy begins in the heart and radiates out into the world – the word *vyana* translates as "expanding" or "expansive". In the following pages you will learn how this energy awakens you emotionally as well as physically. By arousing your desire for personal freedom and stimulating your heart to open, vyana energy makes you more charitable and willing to share your gifts, equipping you to live more harmoniously within your family and your community.

The regions of the body most affected by vyana energy

BREATHING FROM YOUR HEART

If you again imagine that your body is a factory, then your vyana energy would be in charge of the transport department and the postal system. After your prana has taken in energy and oxygen, and your samana has digested and processed it, your vyana energy is responsible for distributing the component materials to appropriate "work stations" around your body. Within your body, the strongest influence of vyana is in your extremities – your arms and legs. Vyana is also your sanitation system, ensuring that waste created at each work station is safely removed.

The first job of your vyana breath is to make sure that sufficient supplies of the three ingredients necessary for metabolism are delivered to your cells – oxygen, digested food and hormones. During gaseous exchange in your lungs (*see pages 20–21*), oxygen from the air you have just inhaled moves into your bloodstream. Yoga teachers tell us that vyana makes sure that the hemoglobin protein in your red blood cells picks up and binds with the oxygen. Vyana energy then ensures that this oxygen-rich blood travels to your heart to be pumped throughout your body. As your blood moves through your arteries, the red blood cells deliver their oxygen to your tissues. Nutrients from your food are absorbed from your digestive system into your blood as it circulates. Vyana ensures that the hormones required for metabolism produced by your endocrine glands are released directly into your bloodstream and circulated to your cells.

ANOTHER REASON TO QUIT SMOKING

The hemoglobin in your red blood cells has 240 times greater affinity for the carbon monoxide you inhale from cigarette smoke than it has for oxygen. If you are a smoker, or live with a smoker, 5–15% of your hemoglobin may be tied to carbon monoxide, even when you are not smoking. You then have less hemoglobin available to carry oxygen to your cells.

WORKING WITH VYANA ENERGY

As you practise the breathing exercises in this chapter, ask yourself the following questions. They can help you to see how to optimize your flow of vyana, and with it your cells' ability to use the nutrients they receive and to get rid of waste.

- *Do I sometimes experience muscle cramp? Could I exercise more to get my circulation flowing better?*
- *How well co-ordinated am I? Could I try a yoga class to see whether this makes me more aware of my movements?*
- *Am I open to the circulation of new ideas? If not, what is restricting me?*
- *How forgiving am I? How can I open my heart to people?*
- *Have I experienced grief in the past? Have I expressed it fully?*
- *Am I overly impulsive? How could I be less reckless?*
- *Do I get "stuck" in ways of behaving? How could I act more generously?*

Simultaneously, vyana assists your blood in waste-removal, picking up toxic by-products of metabolism from cells and clearing them away. Carbon dioxide, for example, leaves your bloodstream and enters your lungs during gaseous exchange, to be exhaled with your out-breath.

When your vyana is free-flowing, all parts of your body are thus well-nourished and dispose efficiently of waste. If your vyana flow is deficient in one area, that body part will receive insufficient oxygen, hormones and nutrients — without adequate oxygen, for example, your body cannot use even vitamin-rich foods. Your removal of waste may also slow, which lowers the efficiency of that body part, leading to health disorders, from muscle cramps to emotional symptoms. To keep vyana healthy, practise the breathing techniques in this chapter and exercise regularly. Moving equips your capillaries — small blood vessels that interact with cells — to maintain a healthy interchange of nutrients and waste products.

VYANA VISUALIZATION:
PROJECTING YOUR VYANA

Vyana has its headquarters at your heart, where your anahata chakra governs your ability to reach out to touch others and to be touched by the joys of life (*see page 25*). When you breathe, this sharing, outward-expanding form of your five subtle energies radiates out from this energetic centre to all parts of your being, governing the circulation of your blood to bring nourishment to and carry waste away from every cell, and also distributing your emotions and thoughts.

Being your "all-pervasive prana", vyana also connects everything in your body with everything in the world – for example, the sense of joy you experience when walking in woods is an expression of vyana, as are any shared experiences with groups of people. To help your vyana flow more freely so that you can express yourself in a meaningful way and live a more spiritually fulfilled life, use the breath-visualization exercise opposite. This exercise also helps to strengthen your vyana should it become weak or deficient – signs of this might be that you feel alienated, alone or "stuck" in ways of behaviour, or a lack of energy or physical coordination. Vyana Breathing aims to open up your heart and lung region, projecting your energy out not only to the rest of your body, but to the world around you and the future that lies ahead of you. In this way, your vyana energy promotes growth at all levels – physical, energetic and spiritual – and also provides an energetic back-up system that can make up for imbalances in your other four forms of prana.

COPING WITH CRAMP

If the muscles in your legs or feet often cramp up, you may have a blockage of vyana. The Vyana Breathing exercise opposite will help to unblock your vyana energy, as will the yoga Sun Salutation sequence demonstrated on pages 58–61.

VYANA BREATHING EXERCISE

This exercise tunes you into the outward-expanding, joyful nature of vyana energy. Start by sitting with your legs crossed (*see pages 35–7*).

1 Sit with your back straight and gently seal your lips. Place your hands on your sternum (breastbone), one on top of the other. Close your eyes.

2 Inhaling deeply through your nose, stretch your arms out as wide as possible at shoulder level. Imagine you are embracing the whole world and visualize positive energy saturating your heart and lungs.

3 At the end of your inhalation, hold your breath, keeping your arms wide open, for as long as you feel comfortable. Visualize your vyana energy as an orange spiral that expands out from your heart to encompass every part of your being, then extends to the horizon and on to infinity.

4 Exhale through your nose, bending your elbows and bringing your hands back onto your sternum. Repeat 5–10 times before relaxing your arms and opening your eyes.

VYANA FABLE:
WAITING FOR THE RIGHT TIME

"Once upon a time, a man practised breathing exercises for many years, but without changing the way he lived – and without attaining any of the wonderful benefits he knew breathing exercises could bring about. Feeling disillusioned, he sought out a teacher, who gave his new student some different, easy breathing exercises. They were preliminary breathing exercises, much simpler than the ones he had been practising hitherto. The teacher also asked the man to eat healthily and live his life according to ethical principles. The student practised diligently, but nevertheless did not stop badgering his teacher to initiate him into more advanced techniques. For the first two years, the teacher met his student's eager requests with the instruction that he must wait.

Gradually, the pupil became accustomed to the exercises and forgot to trouble his teacher for extra instruction. He practised regularly, and lived his life according to the principles set out by his teacher. After several years, the teacher called in his student and asked him to exhale fully and then to inhale deeply. At the end of the inhalation, as he began to retain his breath, the student felt his world expand beyond all boundaries. "

Interpreting the tale

The teacher instructs the student to change his lifestyle, knowing that you must purify mind as well as body in order to receive optimum benefit from breathing exercises, and knowing that such a life-changing process takes time. The teacher also understands the profound benefits of that change if only you can wait for it – vyana energy promotes both physical and spiritual growth. Yoga philosophy teaches that breath is like a spark that has the power to ignite a field of grass. In a few minutes, the entire area can be aflame if the grass is properly prepared – fully-grown and sun-dried. If it is not prepared well or for long enough, the spark will only smoulder and the flame will not spread. Regularly practising breathing exercises – even the most simple ones – arouses the outward-expanding vyana energy that lies dormant within you, if you have prepared your whole self with a healthy lifestyle.

DIRECTING YOUR CIRCULATION

If you notice that part of your body seems to be lacking in energy or is prone to chronic pain, excessive coldness or tension headaches, use your vyana breath along with your powers of visualization to increase energy flow within that region, igniting any latent energy with its energetic spark. Start by lying down or sitting comfortably (*see pages 35–7*).

1 Gently seal your lips and breathe through your nose. Close your eyes and focus your attention on your breath. Let it become rhythmical and full. With each inhalation, visualize your breath expanding to reach the area of difficulty, re-establishing healthy circulation. Don't hold your breath: exhale fully to enable your exhalation to break through unwanted blockages to your energetic flow.

2 If you have difficulty in directing your breath, take your attention to the top of your head and, as you inhale, imagine your vyana breath expanding outward. As you exhale, drop your awareness to your forehead. Inhale and imagine your breath here also expanding outward, then exhale and drop your focus to the back of your head. Repeat, dropping your attention with each exhalation in turn to the base of your brain, your neck and throat, your heart region, your solar plexus, the area around your navel, your kidney or sacral region and, finally, the base of your spine.

3 Now reverse the direction of this sequence, directing your energy up through the same parts of your body with each exhalation, and with each inhalation feeling your vyana energy expanding outward. Then relax.

4 Practise this exercise regularly until you feel able to consciously direct the energy of your breath at will.

THINKING OUTSIDE THE BOX

Regular breathing consists of inhalation and exhalation, but you can train your breath by consciously holding it. This enhances your vyana energy and expands your mental horizons. In Alternate Nostril Breathing (*see page 55*), you hold your breath with your lungs full. The Box Breathing exercise opposite features two different retentions – one after inhaling and the other with your lungs empty.

The latter, an "external" retention, helps to relieve nervous tension and encourage a state of positive quietness. Your blood pressure tends to increase slightly as you inhale and decreases as you exhale, making a retention of breath with empty lungs the calmest part of a breath cycle. Try to practise daily after gently exercising. You may find it helpful to visualize your breath forming a rectangle with its four aspects – in, hold, out, hold. Then watch as your breath morphs into a three-dimensional box since your vyana breath is always outward-expanding.

EXTENDING THE COUNT

Train your lungs by gradually lengthening the time you hold your breath out in Box Breathing (*see opposite*) as you become more advanced:

- *Starter level: inhale 2 – hold in 16 – exhale 8 – hold out 2.*
- *Improver level: inhale 4 – hold in 16 – exhale 8 – hold out 4.*
- *Intermediate level: inhale 4 – hold in 16 – exhale 8 – hold out 6.*
- *Advanced level: inhale 4 – hold in 16 – exhale 8 – hold out 8.*

BOX BREATHING

Before trying this exercise, make sure you have mastered Single Nostril Breathing and Simple Alternate Nostril Breathing (*see page 53*) and Alternate Nostril Breathing (*see page 55*). Sit comfortably (*see pages 35–7*).

1 Sit with your back straight and gently seal your lips. Focus on the sound of your heartbeat. Rest your left hand on your thigh, palm up, and position your right hand in Vishnu Mudra (*see page 54*), palm in front of your face.

2 Close your right nostril with your thumb and inhale through your left nostril for a count of 4. Feel the cool, dry air filling your lungs.

3 Gently pinch both nostrils shut between your thumb and ring and little fingers. Hold your breath for a count of 16. Refocus back to your heartbeat.

4 Release your thumb, keeping your left nostril closed, and exhale through the right nostril for a count of 8. Feel warm, moist air leaving your body.

5 At the end of the exhalation, close both nostrils between your thumb and ring–little fingers and hold your breath out for a count of 2. Imagine a string is pulling your diaphragm up toward your throat (*see Abdominal Lift, page 73*).

6 Release your thumb, keeping your left nostril closed, and inhale through your right nostril for a count of 4.

7 Close both nostrils between your thumb and ring and little fingers, and hold your breath for a count of 16.

8 Release your fingers from your left nostril, keeping your right nostril closed, and breathe out through your left nostril for a count of 8.

9 Close both nostrils and hold your breath out for a count of 2, pulling up your diaphragm as before. This is one round. Aim for 5 rounds daily.

CAUTION: AVOID DURING PREGNANCY: INSTEAD PRACTISE SIMPLE ALTERNATE NOSTRIL BREATHING (*SEE PAGE 53*). AVOID IF YOU SUFFER FROM DEPRESSION OR LOW BLOOD PRESSURE.

WALKING WITH YOUR BREATH

"Blessed is the person who can breathe through his bones."
Indian proverb

Whether you enjoy a brisk morning walk or a leisurely stroll after dinner, a daily outing on foot connects you with the energy of your expansive vyana breath. Moving around expands your world-view – one of the qualities of this breath – while walking conditions your heart and lungs, alleviates stress, stimulates digestion and encourages elimination, including the efficient expelling of stale air from your lungs. Observing your breath as you walk also helps to clear the mind of mental chatter.

Being clumsy or accident-prone may be an indication that you are not fully connecting with your breath. A separation between your mind, body and breath may leave you feeling ungrounded, out of balance, spaced out or emotionally numb. It may also be an indication that you spend too much time "in your head" rather than expanding your energies to connect with those around you – a sign of depleted vyana energy. To reconnect with this breath, make time to walk most days, if possible barefoot over grass or on a beach, and try to practise the Meditative Breath Walking exercise, opposite.

Or try this variation: start with your hands relaxed by your sides. Begin walking at normal pace and gradually lengthen your stride. Taking larger steps will cause your arms to swing out further, accelerating your pace.

MEDITATION MUDRA

This yogic hand position is thought to make you receptive to the input of inspirational energy from the world around you. Place your left hand on top of your right hand at waist level with your palms facing upward.

MEDITATIVE BREATH WALKING

Choose a peaceful spot outdoors for this moving breathing exercise, and practise with bare feet whenever possible.

1 First ground yourself: stand with your feet hip-width apart and parallel to each other with your arms relaxed by your sides. Close your eyes and gently seal your lips. Firmly press both feet into the ground and spread your body weight evenly over them, visualizing a connection with the earth beneath you. Lift your toes and spread them as you replace them on the ground. Hold this pose for a minute or two as you take some deep breaths through your nose.

2 When you feel ready, slowly open your eyes halfway. Fix your gaze on the ground approximately ½m (2½ft) in front of you. Place your hands in Meditation Mudra (*see opposite, below*).

3 Begin to walk, taking slow, short steps. Step forward with your right foot by about 15cm (6in), then take a moment to ground yourself before stepping your left foot forward by the same amount, grounding yourself again. Continue to walk with awareness in this way.

4 Tune each step with your breath: inhale as you lift your foot and exhale as you place it back on the ground. Notice how, after a while, your walking develops a natural rhythm.

5 As you walk, consciously keep your weight balanced over the centre of your body; do not allow it to shift forward or hang back. As your foot touches the ground, feel it rooting itself deeply.

6 Observe how your body becomes involved in the walking action. See how each knee bends, lifts and straightens. Be aware of the movement in your ankles, hips, spine and shoulders. When your attention wanders, keep bringing it back to your breath. Practise for as long as feels right before relaxing and returning to your regular activity.

ENHANCING YOUR SELF-IMAGE

"When exhaling, the stream of air measures about 12 fingers from the nose. When singing, its length increases to 16 fingers; when talking, to 24 fingers. During strenuous exercises, to even more."

Gerhanda Samhita, 84–6

As you begin to practise breathing exercises regularly, you may notice that you can effortlessly complete tasks you used to find difficult. You might find yourself speaking up for what you believe in, even in front of a group. Fear of speaking in public is one of the most common of self-imposed limitations. If you feel apprehensive about contributing in meetings, presenting a report or stating your point of view in public, you may have spent years integrating that fear into your body. By calling on the outward-expanding nature of your vyana breath with the Expansiveness Meditation, opposite, you can begin to dismantle this mental barrier and enhance the way you think about yourself. As you do so, watch how other self-imposed emotional or behavioural barriers break down, and enjoy the liberation of allowing your true self to shine forth.

EXPANSIVENESS MEDITATION

This exercise allows you to physically experience the outward-expanding nature of your vyana breath. Start by sitting comfortably (*see pages 35–7*).

1 Sit with your back straight and gently seal your lips. Close your eyes and take a few deep breaths through your nose. Then, try to stop controlling your breath. Allow it to flow naturally, becoming as deep or as long, as fast or as slow as seems comfortable.

2 Become aware of the parts of your body that are in contact with the ground. Direct your breath in their direction and observe what happens. You may feel as if you are expanding downward or becoming heavy. Or you may feel incredibly light and perhaps even experience a sensation of floating.

3 After a few minutes, shift your awareness to the left side of your body and visualize your energy radiating to this side. Imagine sending your breath into your left leg, waist, arm, neck, cheek and temple. Notice how your body feels – does it seem to be expanding to the left?

4 Become aware of the right side of your body and direct your breath to these body parts. Observe the effects – do you seem to be expanding to the right?

5 Now direct your breath to the rear of your body – not just to your back, but to the nape of your neck and the back of your arms and head. Notice how your body feels – do you have a sensation of expanding backward?

6 Repeat to the front of your body, sending your breath from your belly to your chest and into your arms, throat and face. Observe how your energy radiates toward your front side and how you seem to expand forward.

7 Observe the top of your body, then send your breath into your shoulders, head and scalp. Notice how far your energy radiates up from each part in turn, then feel them all simultaneously expanding upward.

8 Finally, feel your entire body expanding in all directions simultaneously with each breath. If you find it helpful, repeat an affirmation, such as "I am at one," or "Nothing can stop me". Sit quietly before opening your eyes.

OPENING YOUR LUNGS

Strengthening your respiratory system helps you to build a firm physical foundation for your vyana breath, and this allows it to flourish. Use the Sandbag Breathing exercise, opposite, to enhance your respiratory abilities, especially if you find breathing exercises tiring.

The strength of your breathing mechanism depends on how much power you have in the region above your waist. This is the location of your diaphragm – the dome-shaped muscle that divides your trunk into two distinct portions. The upper part comprises your chest cavity, containing your heart and lungs. Below, tightly packed into your abdominal cavity, lie most of your digestive and uro-genital organs. While improving awareness of the way in which you breathe, Sandbag Breathing strengthens this diaphragmatic region and tones your abdominal muscles.

FOODS TO AVOID

Yoga philosophers teach that foods high in sodium, calcium, sugar and saturated fats can inhibit your expansive vyana energy by causing it to contract. Greasy, over-sweet or salty foods as well as dairy produce are also thought to increase mucus, making breathing more difficult. To strengthen your expansive breath, eat more proteins, carbohydrates, omega-3 oils and foods rich in magnesium, potassium, zinc and selenium. Drink plenty of water. Also try to cut down on the following:

• *Junk foods, fast food and ready meals.*
• *Bread and pastries made with white flour.*
• *Soft drinks, especially if very cold or served with ice.*
• *Desserts and sweets made with white sugar, especially after a protein-rich meal.*
• *Overeating (even if the food is healthy).*

SANDBAG BREATHING

Practise this exercise on a firm surface: neither a bed nor soft, upholstered furniture provides the unyielding support your body needs. If you don't have a sandbag, substitute a telephone directory. For one month practise this exercise for 3 days in a row, followed by a day off. It is a good idea to supplement this exercise with inverted yoga postures, such as the Headstand and Shoulderstand (*see pages 102–3 and 146*), or, for newcomers to yoga, with the chest-expanding Fish Pose (*see page 101*).

1 Lie on your back on a firm surface with your legs stretched out. Position your legs apart, with your feet dropping outward, and rest your arms a little way from your sides, palms facing upward and fingers slightly curled.

2 Close your eyes, gently seal your lips and breathe through your nose. Observe your breath. Visualize your abdomen filling and rising with each inhalation, and then watch it empty and fall in your mind's eye as you exhale. Continue for a minute or two, until you feel settled.

3 Place a sandbag (or telephone directory) on your abdomen. Try to continue the same deep abdominal breathing. The weight on your abdomen requires you to work harder to expand your lungs as you inhale. However, it makes exhalation easier. Practise for 5 minutes daily, and then relax. Gradually increase your practice to 10 minutes a day.

CAUTION: IF AT ANY POINT YOU FEEL TIRED OR YOUR BREATHING IS LABOURED, REMOVE THE SANDBAG. AVOID DURING PREGNANCY.

BREATHING WITH COMPASSION

"Your true Self lives in your heart. From there a hundred and one subtle channels radiate outward, each one of them has a hundred branches, every one of these has seventy-two thousand sub-branches — all these are under the diffusing stream known as Vyana."

Prasna Upanishad, 3.7

Your vyana breath is an outward-expanding energy that comes from your heart and empowers you to connect with other people. The Loving-kindness Breathing exercise, opposite, asks you to look into your heart, find your innate compassion and use it to develop an attitude of tolerance and goodwill to all people. You may like to practise it regularly to cultivate a sense of loving expansiveness or to practise at times when you feel upset with someone or are faced with a challenging situation.

Before you begin, simply sit and think about the air you breathe — you inhale more than five million litres (8.8 million pints) of air each year — and how everyone on the planet breathes the same air. You share your supply with all beings, regardless of their genes, social standing or political inclination. During this exercise you experience a heartfelt connection with all of them, but it begins by asking you to focus your vyana energy on generating good feelings toward yourself, for if you do not love yourself, it is impossible to connect with others.

LOVING–KINDNESS BREATHING

Sit comfortably (*see pages 35–7*), loosening your belt and any restrictive clothing. There is no need to visualize yourself on a beach or wooded glen in this exercise: simply be where you are.

1 Sit with your spine straight and gently seal your lips. Rest your hands in your lap in Meditation Mudra (*see page 92*) and close your eyes. Breathe slowly and evenly through your nose, focusing your attention on your heart.

2 Recall a time when you felt content. Breathe deeply as you remember where you were and who you were with. For a few moments mentally re-establish that scene. Now let go of the details, but continue to feel the well-being that accompanies them. You may experience a warm glow in your chest. Send yourself thoughts of peace and happiness, repeating a phrase such as: "May I be happy," "May I be peaceful and content," "May I be filled with loving-kindness." Finish the exercise here for the first few times you practise it.

3 When you feel ready, perhaps after several days, repeat steps 1 and 2, then think of someone who has cared for you and keep the image of that person in your mind while you mentally recite the phrases you used in step 2, now directing the thoughts of well-being toward that person by mentioning his or her name, "May ... be happy," "May ... be peaceful and content," and so on.

4 After a while, begin to include others you love in your thoughts – picture them, evoke the sensation of loving-kindness and recite the same phrases.

5 Once you are able to radiate loving thoughts to these people, extend the warm feelings and words of kindness to beings you feel neutral about – neighbours, colleagues, even animals. Repeat the same phrases for them.

6 Finally, try to extend the feeling further, to people you find difficult or whom you dislike. Again, repeat the phrases. At first your mind may resist extending goodwill to those for whom you feel negativity. This is natural, so when you feel resistance, be gentle and patient with yourself. Practise for 10 minutes daily, breathing deeply, aware of your expansive state of mind.

VYANA EXERCISE SEQUENCE
POSES TO EXPAND YOUR PERSPECTIVE

The Headstand (*see pages 102–3*), considered the "king" of yoga poses, is highly beneficial for expansive breathing. With regular practice, it brings an abundance of radiant vyana energy to your head and upper body. It also rests your heart and circulatory system, which carry out the work of your vyana energy, by inverting your body and allowing gravity to assist the return of the blood to your heart. However, for newcomers to yoga, this pose may be daunting. Build up to it by practising Fish Pose (*see opposite*), which is also noted for its heart-expanding properties. This pose opens your chest, enhancing your breathing capacity and making your emotions feel more "open", too. If you tend to breathe shallowly, have panic attacks or suffer from asthma, you may find that regular practice of this pose helps to strengthen your respiratory system and can ease your breathing problems (however, never practise any yoga poses during an asthma attack).

BUILDING UP A SEQUENCE

If you are new to yoga, start by practising Fish Pose on its own or after the Shoulder Stand and Plough Pose (*see pages 146–7*). Once you can comfortably hold the pose, try the Half Headstand (*see page 102*), and move on to the full pose when you feel confident. This may not be as physically difficult as you imagine and may bring you to face to face with your fears, encouraging you to overcome them – this is your vyana energy in action. If you already practise yoga, it is best to follow these poses in a sequence – start with full Headstand (*see page 103*), coming up into it through Half Headstand, and finish with Fish Pose. If inversions are contraindicated for you (*see caution, page 103*), just practise Fish Pose.

FISH POSE
MATSYASANA

1 Lie on your back on the floor with your legs stretched out straight. Bring your legs and feet together. Place your hands, palms downward, beneath your thighs, one on each side.

2 Bend your elbows, pushing them into the ground. Lift your chest up, then carefully take your head back until the crown of your head rests gently on the floor. Keep your body weight mainly on your elbows. There should be very little weight on your head or neck.

3 Hold the pose for 10–30 seconds. Your chest is wide open in this position, so take advantage by breathing as deeply as possible. To engage your ribcage in the breathing, imagine that your ribs are like the gills of a fish, opening to pull in oxygen. This encourages the circulation of vyana throughout your body. Gradually build up to a 2-minute hold.

4 To come out of the pose: lift your head slightly, slide your head back and lower your back to the ground. Lie here and relax for a few moments.

CAUTION: AVOID IF YOU SUFFER FROM MIGRAINE HEADACHES,
HAVE HAD A WHIPLASH OR OTHER RECENT NECK INJURY,
OR HAVE HIGH BLOOD PRESSURE.

HALF HEADSTAND
ARDHA SIRSHASANA

1 Kneel with your knees and feet together, then sit with your buttocks resting on your heels. Bend your elbows and grasp each elbow with your opposite hand.

2 Bend forward and place your elbows on the ground directly beneath your shoulders. Without moving your elbows, release your hands. Clasp your hands together by gently interlocking the fingers to create a tripod shape with your arms and hands. This will guide your body weight safely onto your elbows rather than onto your head or neck.

3 Place the top of your head on the ground and rest the back of your skull gently against your clasped hands. Straighten your knees without moving your head or your elbows.

4 Slowly walk your feet forward until your hips are directly aligned over your head. Try to keep your arms and head still and make sure that your weight remains on your elbows and not your head. Remember that throughout the pose your elbows should be holding you up.

5 Bend your knees without letting your hips drop. Bring your heels up to your buttocks, keeping your knees bent. Do not jump; come up slowly. Breathe deeply and hold this position – the Half Headstand. Make sure you can comfortably hold it for at least 10 seconds before moving on. This may take some days or even weeks of practice. Until you are ready to move on, come down slowly and rest with your forehead on the ground for a minute.

HEADSTAND
SIRSHASANA

6 When you feel ready to progress to a full Headstand, practise steps 1–5, then, keeping your knees bent, slowly lift them toward the ceiling. Be aware of your elbows, allowing them to support most of your body weight.

7 Gradually straighten your knees, lifting your feet until your body is in a straight line. Keep your weight evenly balanced on your elbows, with very little weight on your head or neck. Breathe deeply and hold the position for as long as you feel comfortable – begin with 10 seconds, gradually building up to 3 minutes. When you are ready, bend your knees and come down slowly. Keep your head down and rest your buttocks on your heels with your forehead on the ground for a full minute before sitting up.

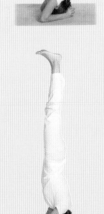

CAUTION: AVOID BOTH POSES IF YOU HAVE HIGH BLOOD PRESSURE, GLAUCOMA, DETACHED RETINA, A COLD OR A BLOCKED NOSE, A WHIPLASH OR OTHER NECK INJURY, AND DURING PREGNANCY. DO NOT PRACTISE INVERTED POSES DURING MENSTRUATION.

CHAPTER 5

YOUR CLEANSING BREATH

UNDERSTANDING APANA

With each out-breath you eliminate stale air from your lungs. The Sanskrit name for your cleansing breath, *apana*, meaning "moving outward from", highlights the nature of this, the penultimate form of subtle energy flowing through your body. It governs the elimination stage of breathing, during which the energies you have taken in with your incoming prana breath are returned to the external environment, along with any waste matter generated by the digestion processes overseen by your samana breath and the circulation of vital ingredients by your vyana breath. Apana energy encourages your body to expel these impurities in the form of urine, solid waste, sweat and menses, and also enables you to release emotional "baggage". In the following pages you will find breathing exercises to boost your apana energy, promoting the release of whatever is toxic, excessive or no longer needed in your life, while conserving all you need to nourish your body, emotions and relationships.

The region of the body most affected by apana energy

CLEARING OUT YOUR SYSTEM

If you again imagine that your body is a factory, then your apana energy would be the shipping department, in charge of transporting out the products created on site and eliminating the waste by-products of the manufacturing process. Within your body, the strongest influence of this expelling energy is in the region below your navel, from where it governs your reproductive organs and urinary tract, your colon and your kidneys (in Traditional Chinese Medicine, kidney energy represents your life-force). As apana energy flows down and outward, it oversees all forms of bodily elimination — sweat, stool and urine, the expelling of semen and menstrual fluid, and the energy that stimulates the birth process, as well as the elimination of carbon dioxide when you exhale.

The impact of apana is felt more strongly in a woman's body than in a man's, in the downward flow which is part of the menstrual cycle and in the expelling energy of childbirth. Menstruation is a healthy expression of downward-flowing apana, and many yoga teachers warn against practising inverted poses when you are menstruating, on the grounds that that they disturb the natural energetic flow of your cleansing breath. However, inversions are recommended at other times of the month in some systems of yoga, such as Iyengar yoga, to improve elimination of excess apana, alleviating problems such as heavy flow and irregular periods.

Ayurvedic practitioners believe that disturbances in the functioning of your apana unbalance the chemical make-up of your body. After you have eaten, for example, gases are released as a natural result of the chemical interaction of food with your digestive enzymes. Some foods, such as raw foods, particularly nuts and seeds, tend to produce more gas than others. Excess gas is also produced as a result of incomplete digestion. It is the job of your cleansing breath to remove these gases. When apana is weak, it may not be able to fulfil this function, leading to an over-abundance of gases, and in particular gases that move up instead

WORKING WITH APANA ENERGY

As you use the breathing exercises in this chapter, ask yourself the following questions. They can help you to see how to optimize your flow of cleansing apana energy.

- *Do I hold onto ideas that are no longer relevant? How could I make my attitudes a little less rigid?*
- *Is my living or work space cluttered because I am unable to let go of things?*
- *Do I finish one project before moving on to the next?*
- *Do I feel stable and balanced? Do I have a sense of my life's purpose?*
- *Does my diet "ground" me? How could I eat more healthily?*
- *Do I chew food thoroughly so that it can be digested fully?*
- *Is my menstrual period regular and pain-free?*
- *Am I often constipated? Could I drink more water during the day to ease these symptoms?*
- *Do I work up a sweat when exercising? If not, how could I work harder physically to sweat toxins from my body?*

of down and out. Ayurveda regards such erratic movement of "air" as a cause of chronic health problems, from high blood pressure, palpitations and heart attacks to respiratory tract disorders and even schizophrenia.

On a more subtle plane, your cleansing breath purges you of negative sensory, emotional and mental experiences. Indeed, whenever you have a clearout of things you no longer need – clothes, work files, even relationships – apana energy is at work. If you find it difficult to assimilate difficult experiences or emotions, the breathing exercises in this chapter can help, offering you the energy you need to eliminate negativity and withdraw from unhealthy situations. Apana is essential for your mind as well as your body to function well, cleansing your entire system and forming the foundation of your immune function on every level.

APANA VISUALIZATION

GROUNDING YOUR APANA

Apana, the cleansing form of your five subtle energies, has its headquarters at the base of your spine. In your body, you experience the energy of apana as the downward pull of gravity that physically connects you to the earth and keeps you feeling emotionally grounded. Your apana is based within your muladhara chakra, which is the energetic foundation of your chakra system (*see page 25*). The role of this chakra is to keep you firmly rooted by releasing energy downward while at the same time energizing you by drawing positive energy up from the earth. Your expelling apana breath also has to work in balance – both with your inward-flowing prana breath (which brings energy into your body; *see pages 40–41*) and with your upward-moving udana breath (which allows you to express yourself; *see pages 130–31*). If your apana fails to strike this balance or even starts to move in the wrong direction, you may feel ungrounded, insecure and fearful, or even "clogged up" and emotionally weighted down. The breath-visualization exercise opposite counters this by encouraging you to engage with the upward flow of your apana from the base of your spine while feeling its grounding energy, which keeps you rooted physically and emotionally.

SPRING CLEANING

When you see it as an expression of apana energy, spring cleaning – or a major clearout at any time of year – takes on a dynamic dimension. As you clean, dust and throw away, appreciate the energetic connection between you and the objects in your home or workplace. A cluttered environment and an excess of possessions that you no longer need or love drain your time and energy by distracting you from what is really important in life. As you get rid of these unnecessary objects, feel your healthy apana energy grounding you and helping to sever an over-attachment to material things.

APANA BREATHING EXERCISE

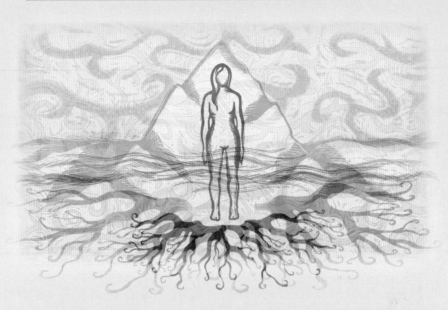

This exercise ensures that your prana and apana energies are balanced and flowing harmoniously, in order to maintain good health and keep you feeling emotionally grounded. It is best, although not essential, to practise barefoot, preferably on a beach or a lawn.

1 Stand with your feet apart, but parallel. Gently seal your lips and close your eyes if you wish. Imagine your body is as firm and grounded as a mountain.

2 Inhale deeply through your nose and imagine drawing the in-breath down to the base of your spine, and then let it drop into your feet.

3 Retain your breath, visualizing your energy continuing to move downward and rooting you deeply into the earth.

4 Exhale through your nose, imagining your breath as a mist lifting from the ground. Watch your mental and emotional toxins drifting away with the mist. Focus on how firmly grounded your feet are as your cleansing breath moves upward through your body. Repeat once or up to 5 times and then relax.

RELEASING TENSION

"He who breathes out with your out-breath [apana] is your true Self,
the eternal essence which is within all things."
Brihadaranyaka Upanishad, 3.4.1

Your autonomic nervous system regulates the vital functions of all your internal organs, including your heart and lungs, as well as your circulatory and glandular systems. It is divided into two systems – your sympathetic and parasympathetic nervous systems.

Your sympathetic nervous system stimulates your organs, gearing up your body for physical action and excitement by increasing your heart rate, blood pressure and muscle tone, which causes your skin to sweat and your pupils to dilate, among other effects. Your parasympathetic nervous system, on the other hand, works in exactly the opposite way. It slows down the functioning of your bodily organs, decreasing your heart rate, blood pressure and muscle tone in order to prepare your body for rest, sleep and digestion.

Stimulation of these two branches of your autonomic nervous system is usually completely involuntary and reflexive. During each breath cycle, your inhalation (governed by prana energy) emphasizes the activity of your sympathetic system, while your exhalation (ruled by apana energy) stimulates your parasympathetic system. Therefore, simply by adjusting your ratio of inhalations to exhalations, you can begin to consciously control your autonomic nervous system to favour the exhalation and apana energy – and therefore parasympathetic activity – whenever you feel the need to let go of built-up tension and enjoy relaxation. Use the Relaxation Breathing exercise, opposite, which emphasizes letting go with the exhalation, at times when it would be useful to release body tension or anxiety, and to feel the energy of apana, your cleansing breath, flowing freely through your system.

RELAXATION BREATHING
SAVASANA

If you have back problems, place a rolled-up towel or cushion under each knee before beginning this exercise.

1 Lie on your back on a firm surface with legs stretched out and wide apart. Rest your arms a little way from your sides, palms up and fingers curled.

2 Close your eyes, gently seal your lips and breathe through your nose, feeling the in-breath swell your abdomen. Focus on your breath, but try not to control it. Instead watch it with your mind's eye, or just listen to it.

3 As you inhale, feel your abdomen rise and imagine your breath saying the word "let". As you exhale, feel your abdomen drop and imagine your breath saying "go". Do not strain or force your breath, simply imagine letting go of a little accumulated worry or strain with each exhalation.

4 Now bring your awareness to your toes. Feel tension here release as a wave of relaxation begins to move up your body. Loosen each part of your legs in turn – first your feet, then your ankles, calves, knees and thighs.

5 Let the wave of relaxation reach your hips, relaxing your abdomen and buttocks, and allow it to slowly move up your back. Feel your tension melting away into the ground and let go of your worries.

6 Feel your chest releasing anxiety and allow your breathing to become gentle. Relax your fingers, hands and wrists, and feel the wave of relaxation move up your arms to your shoulders and neck. Let go of any gripping: there is no need to hold on to anything.

7 Let the relaxation reach your head and soften any hard expressions. Feel your tongue and throat release. Relax your lips, chin, cheeks, eyes, eyebrows, forehead and scalp. Instruct your brain to unwind.

8 Continue to breathe gently, listening to the sound of your in- and out-breaths repeating the words "let ... go". After about 10 minutes, wiggle your fingers and toes. Stretch your arms overhead, giving your body a long, luxurious stretch. Roll to one side before slowly sitting up.

OVERCOMING STRESS

"One who is of a flabby and phlegmatic constitution should first practise the six kriyas [cleansing acts]."
Hatha Yoga Pradipika, 2.21

The strength of the key organs of breathing – your lungs – is directly linked to the strength of your adrenals. These two small glands, one atop each kidney, produce and release regulatory hormones and the chemical messengers that mediate your response to stress. Your adrenal glands are an important part of your body's fight-or-flight response, because they manufacture the hormone adrenaline, which helps you deal with immediate danger, in their inner core, and cortisol, which helps you handle longer term stress, in the outer shell. If your body regularly becomes over-stressed, your adrenal glands may become unable to manufacture the hormones your lungs require for healthy functioning. Adrenal depletion is regarded by Ayurvedic practitioners as a sign of weakened apana energy.

If you suffer from constant fatigue which is not relieved by rest or sleep, complementary health therapists may diagnose adrenal burnout, although not all conventional doctors recognize the term. Other symptoms include a craving for sweet or salty foods, low blood pressure and blood sugar, irritability and depression, impaired digestion and frequent respiratory infections. Sleep will not heal adrenal burnout if your body is unable to regenerate its energy – being chronically overtired interferes with the restorative power of sleep. If the condition worsens, your body may become depleted of vital minerals as well as lack the apana energy it requires to excrete waste products effectively.

SUPPLEMENTS TO BOOST THE ADRENALS AND APANA

The following may strengthen your adrenal glands and enhance apana:

• Daily multivitamin containing calcium, magnesium and zinc.

• 1,000–3,000 mg vitamin C daily.

• 100–400 mg L-Theanine (an amino acid) daily.

• 300 mg vitamin-B complex, including pantothenic acid (vitamin B5), daily.

• Ashwagandha, an Ayurvedic herb that promotes stamina, helps to reduce the effects of stress, and enhances memory and cognitive function. For daily dosage, consult an Ayurvedic practitioner.

• Kelp granules and nutritional yeast, rich sources of nutrients; kelp also assists detoxification. For daily dosages, consult a nutritionist.

• Liquorice root, a tonic used to stimulate adrenal function; for daily dosage, consult a herbalist or nutritionist.

Excessive stress, the underlying cause of adrenal burnout, comes from many sources. Nutritional deficiency is a common one – when under stress, your need for nutrients is greater, yet you may skip meals. A fast-paced lifestyle is another. But this can also be a symptom of burnout – stimulation brings temporary relief from fatigue, but in the long run only further exhausts your body. Stimulants may damage the adrenals, from caffeine and alcohol to anger, loud music and even violent films.

Rebuilding your apana breath is the best place to begin a recovery because apana energy governs your kidneys. Start with cleansing exercises (*see pages 31–2*), then practise the simple breathing exercises on pages 50–55, as well as those in this chapter, to retune your cleansing breath. To nourish your apana energy as your vitality slowly improves, try to eat healthily and at regular times, and reduce sources of stress.

BREATHING FOR NEW LIFE

It is especially important to practise healthy breathing throughout pregnancy, both to oxygenate your baby's body and to prevent the build-up of toxins. Your unborn child releases his or her waste products into your bloodstream, so when you are breathing for two, the cleansing aspect of your breath – apana energy – becomes increasingly important.

However, full, deep breathing can also become increasingly uncomfortable as your baby grows – increased pressure on your abdomen may impede the movement of your diaphragm and other respiratory muscles. Practising cleansing breathing techniques can therefore make you feel more comfortable during pregnancy. It also reduces stress during this time of great change and anxiety by keeping your mind and body calm. Slow-paced Breathing (*see opposite*) can be one of the best ways to prepare for an efficient labour – the more you are able to stay relaxed during childbirth, the less pain you will feel and the more apana energy you will have to help you push out your baby. Apana, your cleansing breath, helps you not only to eliminate the waste your body no longer needs, it helps you to expel whatever is ready to leave your body. Apana is the energy of childbirth.

DEVELOPING BREATH-AWARENESS

If you tune in to your breathing daily during pregnancy, by the time you go into labour, achieving a state of relaxation will be like second nature to your body. Sit on the floor, on a chair or lie on your left side (to boost blood-flow to the baby and help your kidneys to expel waste more efficiently). To get comfortable, place cushions under your knees and behind your back. Close your eyes, listen to the sound your breath makes and feel the air moving through your nose and throat. Then notice how each in- and out-breath affects your shoulders, chest, abdomen and back, and the pressure of your body against the chair or floor.

SLOW-PACED BREATHING

Practise this exercise in different positions, noticing the different sensations as you sit, lie or stand. Rock gently or walk rhythmically while doing this type of breathing if it feels good.

1 Breathing slowly and deeply, start to listen to the sound of your breath flowing in and out. Try counting your breath – "In, 2,3,4,5," "Out 2,3,4,5" – counting up to whichever number feels most comfortable.

2 Now focus your attention on your exhalations. Create a mental link between the words "release tension" and "focus" and your outward-moving, cleansing breath. Direct this thought and your breath into various parts of your body, starting with those that feel tense or restricted.

3 To energize your breathing, continue practising this slow-paced breathing, but visualize your breath as a continuous cycle. Picture energy entering your body as you breathe in and tension leaving as you breathe out.

4 As you continue to inhale and exhale, mentally repeat phrases such as, "Energy in, pain out" or "My breath, mind and body are calm." Alternatively, you may wish to mentally repeat rhythmic phrases on your in- and out-breaths, such as "Healthy baby" or "Be calm, stay calm," splitting the phrases between your in and out-breaths.

5 If it is helpful, add a hissing sound or long, drawn-out "AHHH" to each exhalation. To emphasize the releasing energy of apana, ask your partner or a friend to stroke their hands down your arms or legs as you exhale.

CAUTION: TRY NOT TO HOLD YOUR BREATH DURING PREGNANCY AND CHILDBIRTH.

ROOTING YOUR BREATH

"By regular practice of mulabandha, a union of prana and apana is achieved. Impurities decrease considerably and even the aged become young."
Hatha Yoga Pradipika, 3.65

Mulabandha, also known as Root Lock, is a yogic technique that can vastly improve your overall levels of energy. The exercise stops the downward leakage of energy, having the effect of restraining energy at the base of your torso – the headquarters of your apana – and not allowing it to move downward. At the same time, the technique allows your energy system to act like the roots of a plant extracting nutrients from the earth and drawing them upward. As you practise, you direct your downward-moving apana energy up toward your heart centre (*see page 25*). With practice, you may experience a greater sense of well-being, feel more secure within yourself, and develop courage and inner strength as well as a firm physical foundation for your body.

In men, Root Lock results from contractions of the muscles surrounding the perineum, which lies midway between the anus and the genitals. Women often feel the contraction more strongly in the area surrounding the base of the cervix. The exercise requires concerted, repeated practice, as you may find it difficult to isolate the contractions in such precise areas. If you can't feel the action at first, don't force a movement – practise slowly and gradually to allow your muscles to strengthen as your mental determination builds. This is also an excellent recommendation after giving birth or to strengthen bladder-control.

ROOT LOCK
MULABANDHA

Start by choosing a comfortable sitting position, preferably with your legs crossed (*see pages 35–7*). To make sure that your knees rest on the ground and are lower than your hips, place a cushion under your buttocks if necessary. If you are having trouble understanding which muscles to contract, sit in your chosen position and then briefly place a tennis ball under your perineum. Try to draw your muscles up and away from the ball, then remove the ball before beginning your practice.

1 Sit with your back straight. Close your eyes, gently seal your lips and breathe deeply through your nose for a few moments.

2 When you are ready to begin, take a deep breath in through your nose and hold it. If you are a beginner, try to hold your breath for 5 seconds. As you advance in your practice, gradually increase the time of retention, holding it for as long as you can without straining.

3 While holding your breath, contract your anal sphincter as strongly as possible. Using your physical strength, mental intention and powers of visualization, pull your pelvic floor toward your chest and imagine drawing energy up from your pubis, perineum and anus. Visualize this energy moving up your spine and uniting with other energies around your heart area.

4 When you are ready, release the contraction and exhale through your nose. Wait a few moments and then repeat the exercise. Practise 3–5 times daily. When you have perfected the technique, you may practise it as you hold your breath during Alternate Nostril Breathing (*see page 55*).

CAUTION: AVOID IF YOU ARE PREGNANT OR MENSTRUATING, OR IF YOU SUFFER FROM CONSTIPATION.

CLIMBING THE BREATH LADDER

Contrary to the usual continuous flow of your breathing, the Interrupted Breathing exercise, opposite, contains pauses. As such, it goes against the established order to achieve its effect, just as a scalp massage messes up your hair as it relaxes you. In this exercise, you use your breath to massage your internal organs and to gain greater control over the physical mechanisms that enable you to breathe. This increased control strengthens your apana energy and therefore your ability to eliminate toxins from your body.

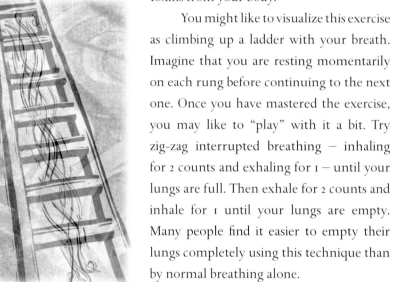

You might like to visualize this exercise as climbing up a ladder with your breath. Imagine that you are resting momentarily on each rung before continuing to the next one. Once you have mastered the exercise, you may like to "play" with it a bit. Try zig-zag interrupted breathing — inhaling for 2 counts and exhaling for 1 — until your lungs are full. Then exhale for 2 counts and inhale for 1 until your lungs are empty. Many people find it easier to empty their lungs completely using this technique than by normal breathing alone.

PROBLEMS WITH COUNTING YOUR BREATH?

You may find yourself getting distracted by the need to count your breath. Perhaps it makes you feel mentally tense or you keep forgetting where you are. There is really no need to be precise, so feel free, if you prefer, to approximate the count.

INTERRUPTED BREATHING
VILOMA

Choose a sitting position (*see pages* 35–7), then practise the first level of the exercise until it feels comfortable, then progress to the second level. If you feel tired or tense, stop and rest by relaxing on your back.

LEVEL 1: STEP WITH YOUR IN-BREATH

1 Sit with your back straight, gently seal your lips and breathe slowly through your nose for a few minutes. When ready to begin the exercise, exhale fully.

2 Inhale for 1–2 seconds, then hold your breath for 1–2 seconds. Do not allow your diaphragm to be loose as you pause, but gently hold it in position.

3 Inhale for another second or two, and then pause. Continue inhaling in this way until your lungs are full. This may involve four or five "steps" with pauses. One complete inhalation of regular relaxed breathing takes about 5 seconds. As you are now interrupting your breath every second or two, it will probably take 15–20 seconds to inhale fully.

5 When you have completed your inhalation, exhale slowly and deeply through your nose, gradually releasing your diaphragm. This completes one round of the exercise. Try to repeat 7–10 times daily.

LEVEL 2: STEP WITH YOUR IN- AND OUT-BREATHS

6 Complete your stepped inhalation as described above. Exhale for 1–2 seconds, then pause and hold your breath for 1–2 seconds. Keep your diaphragm taut during the pause. Then exhale for another second or two, and pause.

7 Continue breathing out in this way until your lungs are empty. This may involve four or five "steps" with pauses. One complete exhalation of regular, relaxed breathing takes about 10 seconds. As you are now interrupting your out-breath every second or two, it will probably take 20–30 seconds to breathe out fully. Try to repeat 7–10 times daily, and then relax.

ELIMINATING NEGATIVE THOUGHTS

One of the best ways to use your cleansing breath is to allow it to wipe away negative patterns of thinking and behaving. You can do this by visualizing your apana energy flowing freely through your spine as you practise a breathing exercise. Visualization is much more than wishful thinking or daydreaming – it allows you to create positive images in your mind. The stronger those positive mental impressions are, the more they help to rid your mind of past trauma and open up mental "space" to allow change and positivity to evolve.

The Spinal Breathing exercise, opposite, cleanses your mind, emotions and nervous system. It is thought to increase the amount of energy flowing through your body and can assist you in reaching a deep state of meditation. When practising this breathing exercise, you may choose to focus your attention on one of the seven subtle energy centres, or chakras, sited along your spine: around the base of your spine, your lower abdomen, solar plexus, heart, throat, forehead and the crown of your head (*see page 25*). Alternatively, you can simply allow the flow of apana energy you visualize to form itself into random shapes, such as a spiral or a figure of eight.

DETOXIFYING PLANTS

Certain houseplants, especially quick-growing varieties with large leaf surfaces, enhance the quality of the indoor air you breathe by producing oxygen, filtering out environmental toxins and humidifying the atmosphere. Cultivate a minimum of two plants per 30 square metres (100 square feet) of room space. A spider plant is particularly useful, or try pot chrysanthemum, dracaena, dwarf date palm, Boston fern, golden pathos, nephthytis, English ivy, aloe vera, philodendron, pothos, rubber plant or weeping fig. Unless you sleep with an open window, remove plants from your bedroom at night, when they absorb oxygen.

SPINAL BREATHING

Start by choosing a comfortable sitting position (*see pages 35–7*). If you practise meditation, then do this exercise just before meditating. Remain seated when you finish and begin your meditation immediately.

1 Sit with your spine straight, balancing your weight evenly on both sides of your body. Gently seal your lips and take a few deep breaths through your nose, until your mind and body feel more peaceful.

2 Close your eyes and begin to mentally observe your breathing. Focus all your awareness inside your body. Visualize your body as empty – imagine that all you have inside your skin is weightless, transparent air. The only physical part of your body is its largest organ, your skin.

3 Now imagine that you are not only breathing through your nostrils – visualize each pore of your skin drawing in air, too. As you inhale through all your pores, visualize your inner space expanding outward. Feel a sensation of gentle expansion, as if you were a balloon. Then, as you exhale, feel your inner space contracting to push out everything you no longer need. Visualize the millions of tiny pores in your skin simultaneously expelling all your toxins and negativity.

4 Within your empty inner space, become aware of a thin, white tube-like thread running from the top of your head to the base of your spine. Trace the course of this tube with your breath. As you inhale, imagine a light moving up the tube. On each exhalation, watch a current of light moving down it. This downward-moving radiance is apana, your cleansing breath.

5 Now focus mainly on your out-breath. With each exhalation, watch the downward-moving light increasing the space it occupies. Permit this torrent of light to carry away all negativity – physical as well as emotional – downward and out from your body. Visualize the toxins exiting through all your pores. Continue practising for 5 minutes, and then relax and gently open your eyes. Repeat every day, gradually increasing the length of your practice as you become more experienced.

APANA EXERCISE SEQUENCE
SALUTING THE MOON

Although apana is the energy of birth in your body, in the universe it is also the energy of sunset and autumn. The Moon Salutation – a lengthy yoga warm-up routine – cultivates the calming and rejuvenating quality of letting go associated with apana, your cleansing breath, while balancing the dynamic energy of prana, your vitalizing breath, within your body. The Moon Salutation sequence works deeply on your mind as well as your body, bringing balance into your life on a variety of levels, physical, psychological and spiritual. Try to practise this sequence at least twice daily. Start the first sequence by bending to the right in step 3 and the second by bending to your left. As you become more experienced, gradually increase the total number of Moon Salutations in your daily practice to 16.

MOON SALUTATION

This routine is best performed as part of an afternoon or evening yoga practice. It is a highly beneficial practice for everyone. Women find it of particular help during menstruation, pregnancy and menopause, as its earthy squats help you to feel more grounded.

1 Begin by standing tall with your feet 5–10cm (2–4in) apart, making sure that your body weight is evenly distributed between both feet. Relax your arms beside your body. Gently seal your lips and take a few deep breaths through your nostrils as you mentally prepare yourself to begin the sequence.

2 Inhaling, raise your arms straight out to the sides and then overhead in a lateral, circular motion. When your hands meet each other, interlock your fingers, then release your index fingers so that they point upward. Try to straighten your elbows and keep your arms behind your ears if possible. Stretch your entire body upward, keeping your chin up and away from your chest.

3 Trying to retain this upward stretch, exhale as you bend toward the right into a lateral stretch resembling a half-moon shape. Push your left hip to the left, but do not allow your body to twist. Make sure that your weight is still distributed evenly between both feet and that your chin is lifted away from your chest. This is Half-moon Pose. Inhaling, return back to the centre. Exhaling, repeat the stretch to the left. Inhale as you again return to the centre.

4 Exhaling strongly, step your right foot into a wide stance, with your feet wider than your hips. Rotate your toes out to a 45-degree angle. Bend your knees and drop your buttocks as far as possible, keeping your back straight and your tailbone tucked under. This is Kali Squat. Do not allow your knees to drop inward: instead keep them over your feet. Simultaneously unclasp your hands, bend your elbows and lower your arms. Bring your elbows below, but in line with, your shoulders (not in front or behind), with your fingers pointing upward and palms facing inward, framing your neck and face.

5 Inhaling, straighten your knees, then pivot your feet so your toes face forward and your feet are parallel to each other. Straighten your elbows and stretch your arms straight out from your shoulders. This is Starfish Pose.

6 Exhaling, turn your right foot and thigh out 90 degrees
to the right and rotate your left foot in slightly. Keeping
your arms extending from your shoulders, stretch your
arms and upper body to the right as far as possible. Then
lower your right hand in front of your right shin or foot.
Keep your arms in a straight line, directing your gaze at
your upper hand. This is Triangle Pose.

7 Inhale and then, exhaling, turn to face the right. Rotate
your back foot until both feet are parallel, with your
right foot in front. Try to keep your hips even. Turn your
entire torso to the right and place both hands on the
ground (if possible) on either side of your right foot. If
you are unable to place your hands on the ground, hold
your right ankle or shin with both hands. Bring your
head down toward your right shin. Try to keep both
knees straight. This pose is Runner's Stretch.

8 Inhaling, bend both knees. Drop your back (left) knee to
the ground, keeping your toes tucked under, and bring
both hands to the floor on either side of your front (right)
foot. Look forward and up. This is the Lunge Position.

9 Exhaling, pivot to face forward, placing both hands in
front of your right foot. Make sure to keep your heel on
the ground and try to keep your right knee directly over
your foot. Rotate your left foot until it rests on the heel
with your toes pointing straight up.

10 Inhaling, walk your hands to the centre. Place both feet flat on the ground and turn your toes out to a 45-degree angle (as in Kali Squat, step 4). Bend your elbows and bring your palms together in a "prayer" position in front of your chest. Try to keep your back as straight as possible as you sit down into this deep squat.

11 Replace your hands on the floor. Exhaling, walk your hands to the left until they are both in front of your left foot. Try to keep your left knee directly over your foot. Then rotate your right foot until it rests on the heel with your toes pointing straight up.

12 Inhaling, pivot to face your left foot, returning to the Lunge Position (*see step 8*). Drop your back (right) knee to the ground, keeping your toes tucked under, and bring both hands to the floor at either side of your front (left) foot. Look forward and up.

13 Exhale as you straighten both knees as far as possible. Make sure your hips stay even and your feet are parallel to each other, with your left foot in front. Try to keep both hands on the ground (if possible) at either side of your left foot. If you are unable to keep your hands on the ground, hold your left ankle or shin with both hands. Bring your head down toward your left shin.

14   Inhaling, raise your right arm and rotate your trunk upward to return to Triangle Pose (step 6). Bring your left hand in front of your left foot or shin. Try to keep your arms in a straight line and direct your gaze toward your upper hand.

15   Exhale and then, inhaling, use your right arm to lead you as you straighten up, returning to Starfish Pose (step 5). Pivot your left foot so that both toes are pointing forward and your feet are parallel to each other. Stretch both arms straight out from your shoulders.

16   Exhale strongly as you turn your toes out to a 45-degree angle and descend into Kali Squat again (as in step 4) by bending your knees and elbows, and sitting down as far as possible. Try to keep your chest up, your back straight and your tailbone tucked under, and check that your knees remain directly over your feet.

17 Inhaling, straighten your arms and legs to come up to a standing position, stepping your feet almost together. Stretch up, trying to straighten your elbows and keep your arms by your ears (as in step 2). Clasp your hands together and release the index fingers so that they point upward.

18 Exhaling, stretch to your right into Half-moon Pose (as in step 3). Inhale as you straighten up back to the centre. Exhaling, stretch to your left, making a half-moon shape. Inhale as you come back to the centre position. Keep your weight evenly balanced on both feet throughout.

19 Exhaling, release your hands and sweep your arms out to the sides and down, coming back to your starting position with your arms relaxed beside your body. This completes one round of the Moon Salutation sequence. In the next round, start by moving toward your left, including bending first to your left in steps 3 and 18.

CHAPTER 6

YOUR EXPRESSIVE BREATH

UNDERSTANDING UDANA

The Sanskrit name of your expressive breath — *udana* — literally means the "air that flies upward". The energy that powers this part of your out-breath begins in your solar plexus and gains strength as it rises up toward your throat. This, the last of your five forms of subtle energy, is transformational. The ancient yoga texts state that, physically, udana energy governs your body's growth, your physical make-up and your ability to stand and move, while emotionally it reveals itself through your enthusiasm and will power and also sustains your voice, giving you the ability to express yourself in a unique way. In the following pages you will find breathing exercises that help you to keep the movement of your expressive breath calm and rhythmic. In doing so, you allow the power of your udana breath to help you to articulate not only who you are now, but your aspirations for who you would like to become.

The region of the body most affected by udana energy

TAPPING YOUR INSPIRATIONAL ENERGY

If, for the final time you imagine that your body is a factory, your udana breath would be the creative director and spokesperson, making sure that your energy is properly channelled into communicating effectively with the outside world. Your expressive breath also directs the energy produced from the fuel you burn into appropriate channels around your body, as well as determining the type of product you manufacture and assessing the quality of its output.

Physically, the ultimate purpose of breathing is to provide your cells with the oxygen they need to burn their fuel – the food you eat. This process of metabolism is sometimes referred to as "internal," or "cellular breathing". When the various nutrients within your food are oxidized in this way, energy is released into your body (along with carbon dioxide, which your cells expel). The primary object of breathing exercises is to stimulate this cellular breathing by enhancing intracellular combustion – all breathing exercises increase your production of internal heat.

Breathing exercises also have a revitalizing effect on your body by enhancing your posture. Udana governs the back of your body and your muscles, and it is udana energy that endows the muscles in your neck with the strength to support the weight of your head. Indeed, only by virtue of the power of udana are you able to stand upright. When your udana energy is free-flowing, you will feel as if you are standing and moving around effortlessly – you may even have a sensation of lightness in your gait, as if you are walking on air.

The breathing exercises in this chapter help to bring your physical body into better alignment with your subtle energy body, too. Yoga teaches that once energy has been released at a cellular level, your expressive breath is free to help you manifest your "self" in whatever way you choose – physical or mental, emotional or spiritual – since udana represents your ability to grow and change in every sphere. Bringing

WORKING WITH UDANA ENERGY

As you use the breathing exercises in this chapter, ask yourself the following questions. They can help you to see how to optimize your flow of transformational udana energy.

- *Do I express myself openly and truthfully? Do my words reflect my thoughts and actions? Or do I waste my expressive breath on small talk and gossip?*
- *Does a tendency to excessive talking distract me and make it difficult to feel peaceful?*
- *Is my voice clear, firm and of good timbre?*
- *Is my life a whirlwind of meaningless activity? How could I better focus my actions?*
- *Do I often feel light-headed? How might I balance this with a sense of being grounded?*
- *Do I regard life as a journey? If so, am I able to explore new directions?*
- *When things are going badly, do I rise to the challenge or sink into despair?*
- *Do I allow myself to grow and change in positive ways?*
- *Do I make the most of available resources? How could I use them more effectively?*
- *How inspired do I feel? Do I have the energy to put my ideas into action?*

your breath under your conscious control by practising these breathing exercises cultivates greater self-awareness as it enhances your udana energy, strengthening your ability to express yourself honestly and to manifest your creativity. This equips you to convey your emotional needs more freely, without fear of what others might think and also without becoming carried away by your feelings.

Your udana breath is the key energy you can use to develop your body and evolve your consciousness, so nurture it with care. The most important breathing exercise in this book may be simply to pause and take a deep breath before you speak or react, not doing anything until you feel able to say only what you need and want to express in the most truthful way you can. Using your breath in this way gives your words great power and makes all your communication more meaningful.

UDANA VISUALIZATION:

ARTICULATING YOUR ENERGY

Within your body, the strongest influence of udana, the expressive, upward-flying form of your subtle energy, is in your head and neck. Here, it has its headquarters at your vishuddha chakra (*see page 25*), the energy centre that governs your ability to communicate, stand up for what you believe in and bring your dreams to fruition. Being the energy of self-expression, your udana breath manifests itself through the sounds you make – every time you exhale, your out-breath creates a vibration that enables you to speak with a unique voice. But udana energy not only empowers your speech, it inspires the thoughts behind your words. Enhancing your expressive energy with the breath-visualization exercise opposite not only helps you to become more articulate, it makes your voice a vehicle for transformational thoughts, helping you to grow and to change for the better. Enhancing your udana energy also helps you to communicate through other media, awakening your hidden creative potential in many fields of expression.

As with all breathing exercises, start slowly and practise regularly. Try not to become too extreme in your practice – excessive udana energy can cause you to talk too much. To guard against this, ground yourself by focusing on your roots in step 2.

CHANTING OM

The Sanskrit mantra OM is made up of three sounds – "AAH", "OOO" and "MMM" – and is considered by yogis to be the "universal sound", the sound you would hear if you put together all sounds, including speech and music. Chanting "OM" is said to have a positive, transformative effect on your nervous system and physical body, and to awaken your latent physical and mental powers.

UDANA BREATHING EXERCISE

In this exercise, the lotus flower represents the power and expressive beauty of your udana energy. Start by sitting comfortably, preferably with your legs crossed (*see pages 35–7*), or, alternatively, stand upright.

1 Keeping your spine straight, close your eyes, gently seal your lips and inhale deeply and fully through your nostrils.

2 Holding your breath, visualize a blue lotus flower blooming at your throat. Imagine its roots sunk deep in mud, and feel the flower's energy flying upward toward the light. Retain your breath for as long as you feel comfortable.

3 Exhaling through your mouth, make the sound "OM" as loudly as you can for as long as you can. Let it start as "AAH" at your solar plexus, move up to your chest in an "OOO" sound as you round your mouth and lips, and vibrate in your face, mouth and throat as "MMM" when you close your lips.

4 Repeat 1–5 times before opening your eyes and relaxing, returning to your regular pattern of breathing.

UDANA FABLE:
THE TORTOISE AND THE HARE

"He who breathes with your up-breath [udana] is your true Self, which is within all things."
Brihadaranyaka Upanishad, 3.4.1

"Once upon a time, in the famous race between the tortoise and the hare, the hare rushed ahead to take the lead. Although the normal breathing of a hare tends to be around 55 breaths per minute, our racer was certainly breathing much faster as a result of his physical exertion. Both running and breathing fast are tiring for the body, so the hare was forced to make frequent "pit stops" to refuel and rest. As a result of his fast, erratic breathing, which necessitated these constant stops and starts, the hare lost the race. The tortoise, on the other hand, started the race slowly and managed to maintain his steady pace throughout. Because he walked rhythmically, rather than running, he had no need to increase his normal rate of breathing by much – tortoises tend to take around 3–5 breaths per minute. This enabled him to complete the course without stopping – and to win the race."

Interpreting the tale

If you look at your life, would you stay that you rush around like the hare? Is your life composed of ups and downs or stops and starts? Or are you more regular in your habits, not allowing yourself to become over-tired and tending to cope with trials without making a fuss, like the tortoise? There is a theory in India, which of course cannot be proven, that your lifespan is not measured by the number of years, but by the number of breaths you take. Therefore, if you speed up your breathing by making it fast and shallow, you use up your allotted breaths faster and shorten your time on Earth. A person of average health takes around 18 breaths per minute when awake — or 1,080 breaths per hour. Therefore, during a 24-hour day, you take in around 24,000 breaths (your breathing slows during sleep). At just under 9 million breaths per year, you will have taken over 600 million breaths by the age of 70. An excitable person who breathes more quickly probably reaches that number of breaths much earlier. The hare, with his 55 breaths per minute, has a life expectancy of 10 years, while the tortoise with his 3—5 breaths per minute lives some 193 years (see chart of comparisons below).

By using the energy of udana, your expressive breath, you can learn to slow your rate of breathing and to direct the breaths you take in a more positive way. With regular practice of the breathing exercises in this chapter, you will be able to take fewer breaths and become better equipped to put each breath to healthy use, since udana energy regulates your cognitive skills as well as controlling the tension of your vocal cords to help you to express yourself.

RELATIVE RATES OF BREATHING AND LIFESPAN

	Approx. number of breaths per minute	*Average life expectancy*
Hare	55	10
Human being	15—18	70
Tortoise	3—5	193

BREATHING FOR SUCCESS

Ujjayi Breathing is an expression of your upward-flying udana energy – the Sanskrit prefix *ud*, which is part of both the words *ujjayi* and *udana*, signifies an upward expansion, while *jaya* means "victory", indicating how harnessing your udana energy can help you to succeed in all your endeavours. The characteristic element in Ujjayi Breathing is the partial blocking of your glottis, the flap at the back of your throat (just behind your Adam's apple) which facilitates speech and closes when you gargle to prevent water going down your throat. Constricting your glottis amplifies the regular sounds of breathing and, when done properly, creates a soft vibration that soothes your nerves and calms your mind.

Before you begin the exercise opposite, practise contracting the muscles of your neck, around your collarbones, by drawing in the inside of your throat as you inhale – Ujjayi Breathing is also known as "throat friction". Notice how this slight tension acts like a wind-breaker to incoming air, producing a continuous sound without using your vocal cords or soft palate (unlike snoring). Practise contracting these muscles until you hear a sibilant "SSS" sound as you inhale and an aspirant "HHH" during exhalation – you may sound rather like Darth Vadar!

UJJAYI BREATHING DURING YOGA EXERCISES

Some yoga traditions advocate practising Ujjayi Breathing while you perform postures. Ujjayi can also be practised while you are meditating, walking or running. If you practise in this way, never hold your breath — simply contract your glottis, allowing your breath to come and go continuously. Try to keep your inhalations and exhalations even to balance your prana and apana. You may increase the rhythm of your breathing at the peak of a pose or during Sun Salutation sequences (see pages 58–61). As you advance in each pose, your breathing tends to accelerate of its own accord, and it is best not to resist this.

UJJAYI BREATHING
UJJAYI

This breathing technique provides a powerful stimulation to your udana energy. It can also improve your speaking voice and stoke your digestive fire, boosting the exchange of gases and prana. Yoga teachers recommend this exercise for problems of excess mucus, coughs, fever, asthma, consumption, low blood pressure and respiratory ailments. By invigorating your nervous system, it reduces depression and is considered a great aid to meditation. Start by sitting comfortably (*see pages 35–7*).

1 Sit with your back straight and your thorax thrust slightly outward, like the chest of a warrior. Rest your left hand on your left knee, palm facing upward, and then position your right hand in **Vishnu Mudra** (*see page 54*) and hold your palm in front of your face.

2 Gently seal your lips and partially close your glottis by contracting the muscles around your collarbones (*see opposite*). Inhale slowly through both nostrils. You should hear a continuous low, soft and uniform sound.

3 At the end of your inhalation, gently pinch both nostrils shut between your right thumb and little and ring fingers. Hold your breath for as long as is comfortable. If you have been practising breathing exercises for some years, you may like to apply both the **Chin Lock** (*see page 143*) and the **Root Lock** (*see page 117*) during your retention.

4 When you are ready to exhale, release the fingers on your left nostril (and at the same time release the Locks, if you are using them). Then slowly and silently exhale through your left nostril, keeping your right nostril closed with your thumb. This completes one round.

5 To begin with, practise 5 rounds, gradually increasing to 20 rounds in each sitting, and then relax. If you would like to practise this exercise further, it is best to seek the guidance of an experienced yoga teacher.

YOUR UPWARD-FLYING BREATH

"Fill in the air rapidly, making the sound of a male bee, practise retention and again exhale it, making the sound of a female bee humming. The great yogis by a constant practice of this feel an indescribable joy in their hearts."

Hatha Yoga Pradipika, 2.68

Bumblebee Breathing (*see opposite*) stimulates and purifies your throat chakra, your energetic centre of communication and the seat of your udana breath. Yoga texts explain that this exercise frees your mind from inner "chatter" and the urge to gossip, prepares you to discover your true voice and equips you to speak in a more measured way – all important properties of your udana energy. With practice, this breathing exercise is said to also improve your concentration, memory and confidence, and you may find that it develops in you a greater willingness to listen and an ability to communicate at a more profound level. Bumblebee Breathing also brings an experience of great inner peace.

This humming breathing exercise is recommended if you are a singer, actor, teacher or public speaker – or if you would simply like to improve your speaking and communication skills for use at work, at home and in social situations. Yogis who practise the exercise on a regular basis report that their speaking voice sounds sweeter and more melodious.

If, when starting this exercise, you have trouble making the bee-like sound, begin by practising the humming exhalation on its own. Simply inhale deeply and repeat a word that ends with an "m", such as "palm", "calm", "hum" or "OM". Draw out the final "m" sound for as long as you can. Humming as you breathe out helps you to regulate your breathing pattern and encourages an extended exhalation, both important components of the exercise opposite.

BUMBLEBEE BREATHING
BHRAMARI

On beginning this exercise, you may feel a slight increase in body temperature, as it quickens your blood circulation. If you are prone to throat problems, note whether regular practice fosters an improvement. Start by choosing a comfortable sitting position (*see pages 35–7*).

1 Sit with your back straight, then make sure that your abdomen and chest are unobstructed and free from tension. Rest the palms of your hands on their respective knees.

2 Gently close your mouth and lips, then tighten the back of your throat. Try to remember to keep your head erect and your neck muscles relaxed.

3 Inhale strongly through both nostrils, vibrating your soft palate and making a snoring sound that energizes your throat. Some people liken this to the sound you make when you are clearing your throat. Yoga texts compare it to the buzzing of a large black bumblebee, or a male bee.

4 Hold your breath for a few moments – for as long as you feel comfortable doing so. During this brief breath retention, think about the upward-flying udana energy in your body.

5 When you are ready, exhale through both nostrils, making the high-pitched humming sound, "MMM". Ancient yoga texts compare this sound to the buzzing of a small honey bee – or a female bee. Try to exhale all the air from your lungs.

6 Repeat the exercise 3–5 times, feeling the vibration in your throat, mouth, cheeks and lips. You may like to experiment by buzzing at different pitches to see how they affect your energy.

7 After you have finished, close your eyes and breathe silently. Sit quietly for 3–10 minutes, noticing the effect the humming has had on your mind.

THE SOUNDS OF SILENCE

"The breath goes out making the sound 'HAM' and comes in producing the sound 'SO'.
You repeat the mantra 'HAMSO' 21,600 times every twenty-four hours."
Yoga Chudamani Upanishad, 31-32

You can purify and calm your mind by limiting your intake of sensory impressions just as some people cleanse their bodies by fasting. Sealing Off Your Senses (*see opposite*) is a technique that frees you from external stimulation so you can focus on the sound of your breath, which strengthens your ability to control your udana. In the profound silence that ensues, you hear your breath repeat the syllables "SO" on the in-breath and "HAM" on the out-breath. *So-ham* is a profound Sanskrit mantra that links you with all other creatures that breathe, since their breath makes the same sound. The literal meaning of *So-ham* is "I am." If you reverse the syllables by listening to the exhalation first, you hear *hamso* or *hamsa*, Sanskrit for "soul" and "swan", symbol of the divine spirit.

HEARING INNER SOUNDS

If you block off external stimulation, you sometimes hear *anahata* (literally "un-struck") sounds that have no physical source, referred to in Western philosophy as the "music of the spheres". In sense-deprivation exercises you might like to listen for such sounds, which may manifest as:

- *Tinkling wind chimes*
- *Bells ringing*
- *The blowing of conch shells*
- *Lute-like sounds*
- *Chinking cymbals*

- *Flute music, heard most often early in the morning*
- *A drum beating*
- *Distant thunder rumbling.*

SEALING OFF YOUR SENSES
SHANMUKHI MUDRA

In Sanskrit, *shan* means "six" and *mukhi,* "face". In this exercise, you close the six "gates" to the face by which you recieve external stimuli – two ears, two eyes, nose and mouth. At first you may find that the sensory deprivation makes this exercise more challenging than others. But those who persevere often report a sensation of deep peace and well-being. Start by choosing a comfortable sitting postion (*see pages 35–7*).

1 Sit with your back straight. With your mouth closed, become aware of the natural movement of your breath in and out through your nostrils.

2 When ready, bring both hands to your face. Gently insert the tips of your thumbs into your ears. Use your index fingers to carefully close your eyelids (without applying pressure to your eyeballs). Rest your middle fingers softly on each side of the bridge of your nose. This reduces your intake of breath, but do not cut it off completely. Close your mouth by placing your ring fingers on your upper lip and your little fingers on your lower lip (*see image* A).

A

3 Breathing lightly through your nose, turn your focus inward and listen to the sound of your own breathing. Notice how, as you inhale, your breath utters the sound "SO", and how with each exhalation it spontaneously repeats the syllable "HAM".

4 As a beginner, practise this for at least 5 minutes, focusing your mind back on the syllables "SO" and "HAM" each time you become distracted. Then lift your hands away from your face and relax them, and gently open your eyes. With practice, gradually increase your sitting time to 20 minutes.

PRESERVING POSITIVE ENERGY

"Contract the throat and press the chin firmly against the breast (four inches from the heart). This is jalandhara bandha: it prevents premature aging and death."

Hatha Yoga Pradipika, 3.70

Yoga breathing exercises combine the practice of breath control with various "locks" (bandhas) and hand positions (mudras) that "seal in" your energy. Without the locks, the breathing exercises are considered incomplete. Although the Sanskrit word *bandha* is usually translated as "lock", it also means "to tie", "to control", "to block", "to hold", "to join" and "to contract". In breathing exercises, it usually refers to muscular contractions that help you to focus your energy.

The Chin Lock exercise, opposite, blocks the upward movement of udana, your expressive breath, at one of your body's most important acupressure points – your throat. In Sanskrit, the word *jala* means "net" or "network", referring here to your spine and the network of nerves that connect to your brain at your neck, the centre of your udana energy. *Dhara* denotes "upward pull" – this exercise exerts an upward pull on your spinal cord and nerve centres, which in turn work on your brain. Applying Chin Lock also helps you to bring your lungs and cardiovascular system under conscious control and calms your heartbeat, enabling it to establish a strong and steady rhythm. Chin Lock is valued by yogis for helping to stabilize your hormones and your rate of metabolism by energizing the thyroid gland at the front of your neck.

Energetically, by applying this lock as you retain your breath, you focus your udana breath in your throat region, stimulating your vishuddha chakra (*see page 25*). This helps to remove energy blockages or imbalances, allowing impulses to pass back and forth along the chakra system between your heart and your mind so that your thoughts can be clearly expressed as speech using your udana breath.

CHIN LOCK
JALANDHARA BANDHA

This is perhaps the most important of all the bandhas, or energy locks. Physically, it prevents the movement of air into your throat and Eustachian tubes (leading to your ears) when you hold your breath. If you are having difficulty in understanding how to do it, first practise Shoulder Stand (*see page 146*) and then incorporate Chin Lock into your breathing exercises once you have mastered this inverted pose. Start by choosing a comfortable sitting position (*see pages 35–7*).

1 Sit with your spine upright. Gently seal your lips and inhale fully through your nose. Notice how, at the end of your inhalation, your breastbone rises slightly.

A

2 At the end of your inhalation, just before starting to hold your breath, place the top of your tongue flat against the roof of your mouth. Swallow gently, causing your tongue to slide back, creating a vacuum at the back of your throat. Drop your head forward so that your chin touches your collarbones and blocks your throat. Rest your chin in your jugular notch – the V-shaped hollow at the base of your throat where your collarbones join (*see image A*).

3 Hold this position for as long as you can hold the breath in your lungs.

4 When you feel ready to exhale, first relax your throat, then return your head to an upright position. Relax your tongue and exhale fully, relaxing and returning to your regular breathing.

CAUTION: ONLY PRACTISE THIS LOCK DURING A FULL RETENTION OF BREATH. AVOID DURING PREGNANCY AND IF YOU SUFFER FROM DEPRESSION OR LOW BLOOD PRESSURE.

FLOATING ON AIR

"Having filled the inner part of the abdomen completely with air,
the practitioner moves upon the waters like a lotus leaf."
Hatha Yoga Pradipika, 2.70

The energy of your udana breath can make you feel as if you are floating on air, and the Floating Breath exercise opposite allows you to tune into this as you float in water. The technique uses the upward-growing lotus as a symbol of the upward-moving energy of your expressive breath. The lotus is a water plant that has its roots in mud but grows upward toward the light – from the muck emerges something of great beauty and delicacy that is unaffected by its watery environment, for although the plant floats on water, the leaves never get wet or soggy. Practising the Floating Breath exercise opposite is said by yogis to help amplify your udana breath so that you develop a similar ability to move about in the world but remain untainted by its negativity and stressful elements.

Floating Breath is a most unusual breathing exercise. Instead of filling your lungs with air, you swallow the air and fill your belly with it. You literally drink the air slowly, as if gulping water down into your stomach. If you were to tap your stomach when it is filled with air, you would hear a peculiarly tympanic (drum-like) sound.

Like other breathing exercises, Floating Breath is usually practised in a regular sitting position. However, you can practise it in various yoga postures, including Fish Pose (*see page 101*), and you can also do it in water, either in a swimming pool or in the bath. By keeping your stomach inflated, the exercise allows you to float in water for an indefinite time.

Once mastered, Floating Breath is a valuable de-stressing tool and you may wish to combine it with relaxing baths, such as mineral-salt baths or hot baths. It can also help if you need to release excess acidity from your stomach or to relieve hunger pangs if you are fasting.

FLOATING BREATH
PLAVINI

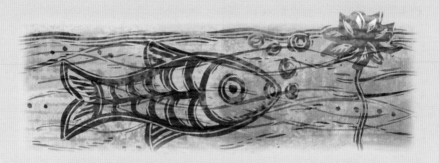

This routine is best practised on an empty stomach, preferably after physical exercise and other breathing techniques. Do it in your usual practice area, at the side of a swimming pool or next to your bath tub.

1 Sit comfortably. Open your mouth to inhale. When you feel the air at the back of your throat, gulp it down, as if swallowing food. Alternatively, fill your mouth with air, close it, pinch your nostrils shut, puff out your cheeks and swallow. Repeat 5 or 6 times, until your stomach is full of air.

2 Continue to sit, or at this point move into a bath or a pool and recline in the water. If you have space, cross your legs and hold your feet if you can. Drop your head back, close your eyes, breathe gently, relax and float with the aid of your air-filled stomach. Visualize your body and mind as being as light as a feather, or like a delicate lotus flower drifting unsullied above the mud in which it is rooted.

3 When you are ready to release the air, burp it up. Assist the process by practising the Abdominal Lift (*see page 73*) or by hiccuping, and then relax.

4 Repeat again, if desired, but build up your practice very gradually.

CAUTION: AVOID IF YOU HAVE STOMACH-ACHE, SUFFER FROM
INTESTINAL GAS PAINS OR ARE PREGNANT.

UDANA EXERCISE SEQUENCE:
POSES TO GROUND EXPRESSIVE ENERGY

The following poses stimulate your throat, easing energy blockages that might prevent you from expressing yourself fully. They also bring balance to your neck, soothing and grounding your udana energy. This is helpful if you tend to be too expressive – for example, if you talk too much, worry excessively or have an overactive mind that results in insomnia.

BUILDING UP A SEQUENCE

It is best to practise these poses in a sequence. First let Shoulder Stand prepare you energetically and mentally to shoulder responsibilities, then use Plough Pose to stretch your spine and broaden your self-expression. A good counter-balance to these poses is Fish Pose (*see page 101*). Finish with Lion Pose to build the courage you need to express your potential. If the first two poses are not for you (*see caution opposite*), go straight to Lion Pose.

SHOULDERSTAND
SARVANGASANA

1 Lie on your back, legs together, and lift them up by 90 degrees.

2 Place your hands on your buttocks, one on each side. Walk your hands up your back, lifting yourself until your body is as straight as possible from shoulders to feet and your weight rests on your upper arms, elbows pointing away and fingers toward your spine.

3 Relax your calves and feet. If you are a beginner, hold for up to 10 seconds. Gradually increase the time, building up to 3 minutes.

4 Drop your legs behind your head, halfway to the floor and either do Plough Pose or place your palms on the floor and roll down.

PLOUGH POSE
HALASANA

1 From Shoulder Stand, exhale as you drop one foot to the ground behind your head. Inhale as you raise your leg. Repeat with your other leg.

2 Try to drop both feet to the ground behind your head as you exhale. If your toes touch the ground, flatten your palms on the floor behind your back. If your feet do not reach the floor, keep your hands on your back for support.

3 Try to hold the position for 10 seconds, breathing steadily. Gradually build up to 1 minute in the pose, and then work up to a 3-minute hold.

4 When ready, slowly roll down, keeping your arms and head on the ground while lowering each vertebra separately. When your back is on the floor, lower your legs and relax for a minute before progressing to Lion Pose.

CAUTION: AVOID BOTH INVERSIONS IF YOU ARE MENSTRUATING, PREGNANT OR HAVE A NECK INJURY.

✽

LION POSE
SIMHASANA

1 Sit on your heels, resting your hands lightly on your thighs. Inhale deeply through your nose.

2 Exhale strongly through your mouth, making a roaring sound. As you do so, "spring" your upper body forward – straighten your arms, stiffen your body, make "claws" with your fingers, stick your tongue out as far as possible and bulge out your eyes.

3 Relax and repeat the "pounce" 2–3 times. Then relax completely.

HEALTH AND PERFORMANCE PROGRAMS

If breathing exercises are to have a noticeable effect on your life, three things are absolutely essential: practice, practice and more practice! If you find the sheer variety of exercises in this book daunting, start with these simple programs selected to meet common health needs and boost your performance at work and in sport. The suggestions are not a prescription, more a starting point – feel free to experiment, drawing up a routine to suit your body, mood and lifestyle. Before beginning a routine of breathing exercises, it is a good idea to assess your breath and posture (*see pages 28–30*), and cleanse your respiratory system with a neti pot (*see page 31*) or the Purifying Breath (*see page 32*). Practise on an empty stomach and allow yourself sufficient time to complete each exercise.

A.D.D. (ATTENTION DEFICIT DISORDER)/A.D.H.D. (ATTENTION DEFICIT HYPERACTIVE DISORDER)

Try to keep children to a schedule, with set times for meals and sleep, homework and exercising (try also to cut down on TV and computer time). Practise these daily:

- Counting Backward (*see page 47*) for 3–5 minutes. You can turn this into a memory game – count 4 elephants, 3 monkeys, 2 tigers, 1 pig all on one exhalation.
- For older children, introduce Simple Alternate Nostril Breathing and Alternate Nostril Breathing (*see pages 53 and 55*).
- 4–6 rounds of Sun Salutation (*see pages 58–61*), then Lion Pose (*see page 147*).

ANGER

When you feel anger building, focus on the breath at your nostrils or try 2:1 Breathing (*see page 51*). If prone to anger, read pages 46–7 and begin a daily routine including:

- 10–20 minutes sitting Watching your Breath (*see page 27*).
- At least 2 rounds of Moon Salutation (*see pages 122–7*).
- 3 rounds of Purifying Breath (*see page 32*).

- If new to breathing exercises, practise 10 repetitions of Single Nostril Breathing, then Simple Alternate Nostril Breathing (*see page 53*). After perfecting the latter, try 10 rounds of Alternate Nostril Breathing with a full retention (*see page 55*).

CAUTION: AVOID SUN BREATHING AND ANY OTHER FORM OF HEATING EXERCISE.

ANXIETY/PANIC ATTACKS

Anxiety is often about the future, so ground yourself in the present by becoming aware of your breath and trying 2:1 Breathing (*see page 51*). Do the following daily, which also helps with pre-exam distress and calms before homework or revision:

- 10–20 minutes sitting Watching your Breath (*see page 27*), with your hands in Chin Mudra (*see page 34*), fingers pointing down, to help you feel more grounded.
- 6–12 rounds of Sun Salutation (*see pages 58–61*), then follow by holding Fish Pose (*see page 101*) for 1–3 minutes.
- If new to breathing exercises, begin with 10 rounds of Single Nostril Breathing, then of Simple Alternate Nostril Breathing (*see page 53*). When you have perfected the latter, try Alternate Nostril Breathing with a full retention (*see page 55*).
- Then add 5–10 rounds of Ujjayi Breathing (*see page 137*).
- Finish with Lion Pose (*see page 147*).

CAUTION: AVOID THE FIVE TIBETAN RITES, SUN BREATHING AND ANY OTHER FORM OF HEATING EXERCISE.

ASTHMA/SKIN DISORDERS

It is particularly important to cleanse your respiratory system with a neti pot (*see page 31*) and at least 3 rounds of Purifying Breath (*see page 32*), then do these daily:

- If new to breathing exercises, practise 10 rounds of Single Nostril Breathing, then of Simple Alternate Nostril Breathing (*see page 53*). After perfecting the latter, try 10 rounds of Alternate Nostril Breathing with a full retention (*see page 55*).
- Then add 5–10 rounds of Ujjayi Breathing (*see page 137*).
- Regulate your breath with 6–12 rounds of Sun Salutation (*see pages 58–61*), then hold Fish Pose (*see page 101*) for 1–3 minutes.
- Investigate Butyenko Method and try a regular practice of one or more of the following: Alexander Technique, Conscious Breathing or yoga (*see page 157*).

CAUTION: DO NOT DO BREATHING EXERCISES DURING AN ASTHMA ATTACK.

CHRONIC FATIGUE/LACK OF ENERGY/LETHARGY

You may have exhausted your resources with too frequent "fight or flight" reactions. Read pages 112–13 to trace possible causes and add these exercises to a daily routine:

- 6–12 relaxed rounds of Sun Salutation (*see pages 58–61*); rest between rounds.
- 3 gentle rounds of Purifying Breath (*see page 32*).
- If new to breathing exercises, practise 10 rounds of Single Nostril Breathing, then of Simple Alternate Nostril Breathing (*see page 53*). After perfecting the latter, try 10 rounds of Alternate Nostril Breathing with a full retention (*see page 55*).
- Then add 5–10 rounds of Ujjayi Breathing (*see page 137*) followed by 5 rounds of Interrupted Breathing (*see page 119*).
- 3–5 rounds of Bumblebee Breathing (*see page 139*).

CIRCULATORY ISSUES

Read pages 83–5, asking yourself the questions on page 85, and try the Vyana Visualization (*see pages 86–7*) as well as the following daily exercises:

- On alternate days practise 6–12 rounds of Sun Salutation (*see pages 58–61*) or the Five Tibetan Rites (*see pages 78–81*, building up to 21 repetitions of each exercise).
- Hold Headstand (*see page 103*) for 1–3 minutes (avoid if you have high blood pressure).
- 5 rounds of Purifying Breath (*see page 32*) (avoid with high blood pressure).
- If new to breathing exercises, practise 10 rounds of Single Nostril Breathing, then of Simple Alternate Nostril Breathing (*see page 53*). After perfecting the latter, try 10 rounds of Alternate Nostril Breathing with a full retention (*see page 55*).
- Then add 5–10 rounds of Ujjayi Breathing (*see page 137*) followed by 5–10 rounds of Sun Breathing (*see page 71*).
- 2–3 rounds of Bumblebee Breathing (*see page 139*).

CONCENTRATION

When you need greater focus, stop and try Interrupted Breathing, including the "zig-zag" variation (*see pages 118–19*). To enhance concentration do these daily:

- Sit for at least 10–20 minutes of Watching your Breath (*see page 27*).
- 6–12 rounds of Sun Salutation (*see pages 58–61*), then follow by holding Headstand (*see page 103*) for 1–3 minutes.

- 3 rounds of Purifying Breath (*see page 32*).

- If new to breathing exercises, practise 10 rounds of Single Nostril Breathing, then of Simple Alternate Nostril Breathing (*see page 53*). After perfecting the latter, try 10 rounds of Alternate Nostril Breathing with a full retention (*see page 55*).

- Box Breathing (*see page 91*).

DEPRESSION

To combat mild depression, try to amplify your breathing – increasing the amount of oxygen reaching your lungs, blood and cells has an uplifting effect. Begin by reading pages 46–7 and try to take 1–2 yoga classes each week. Practise the following daily:

- Five Tibetan Rites (*see pages 78–81*), building up to 21 repetitions of each exercise.

- Headstand (*see page 103*) and/or Fish Pose (*see page 101*) when you would like to change your perspective on the world.

- If new to breathing exercises, practise 10 rounds of Single Nostril Breathing, then of Simple Alternate Nostril Breathing (*see page 53*). After perfecting the latter, try 10 rounds of Alternate Nostril Breathing with a full retention (*see page 55*).

- Then add Ujjayi Breathing (*see page 137*), Sun Breathing (*see page 71*) and Interrupted Breathing (*see page 119*).

- Floating Breath (*see page 145*) tends to cultivate a feeling of lightness of being.

- Bumblebee Breathing (*see page 139*) lifts the higher energy centres (*see pages 24–5*).

DIGESTIVE PROBLEMS

Focus on your nourishing breath (*see pages 62–81*) and try to eat your main meal when your digestive fire is strongest – at noon, chewing well. To remove excess mucus from your system, try to cleanse with a neti pot daily (*see page 31*), practise diaphragmatic breathing (*see pages 28–30*) and practise the following exercises daily:

- Purifying Breath (*see page 32*) with Abdominal Lift (*see page 73*).

- If new to breathing exercises, practise 10 rounds of Single Nostril Breathing, then of Simple Alternate Nostril Breathing (*see page 53*). After perfecting the latter, try 10 rounds of Alternate Nostril Breathing with a full retention (*see page 55*).

- Sandbag Breathing (*see page 97*) builds the abdominal muscles that aid digestion.

- For problems with your acid-alkaline balance, try Hissing Breath (*see page 77*).

- Abdominal Lift and Fire Purification (*see page 73*).

DYSLEXIA

First read pages 52–7, then add the following exercises to your daily routine:

• 6–12 rounds of Sun Salutation (*see pages 58–61*), trying to stay aware of whether you are moving to the left or the right.

• Alternate Nostril Breathing (*see page 55*) to connect the right and left hemispheres of your brain. If new to breathing exercises, first try 10 rounds of Single Nostril Breathing, then of Simple Alternate Nostril Breathing (*see page 53*) before building up to 10 rounds of Alternate Nostril Breathing with a full retention (*see page 55*).

• 3–5 minutes Sealing Off Your Senses (*see page 141*).

GRIEF

First read pages 46–7 and pages 50–51, then practice 2:1 Breathing (*see page 51*) and add the following exercises to your daily routine:

• 6–12 rounds of Sun Salutation (*see pages 58–61*) followed by a 1–3 minute Headstand (*see page 103*) each morning.

• If new to breathing exercises, practise 10 rounds of Single Nostril Breathing, then of Simple Alternate Nostril Breathing (*see page 53*). After perfecting the latter, try 10 rounds of Alternate Nostril Breathing with a full retention (*see page 55*).

• Then add Sun Breathing (*see page 71*) to put the "spark" back into your life.

• Spend 10–20 minutes Walking with Your Breath (*see pages 92–3*) each morning and/or evening to get yourself moving and ready to move on.

• Loving-kindness Breathing (*see page 99*) – taking care to mention the person whom you are grieving for.

HAY FEVER/ALLERGIES

If symptoms such as sneezing and a runny nose make breathing exercises difficult, cleanse with a neti pot (*see page 31*) daily and at least 3 rounds of Purifying Breath (*see page 32*) each morning to keep your nasal pasages free from blockages. Try to avoid mucus-forming foods and add the following exercises to your daily routine:

• If new to breathing exercises, practise 10 rounds of Single Nostril Breathing, then of Simple Alternate Nostril Breathing (*see page 53*). After perfecting the latter, try 10 rounds of Alternate Nostril Breathing with a full retention (*see page 55*).

• Then add 5–10 rounds of Ujjayi Breathing (*see page 137*).

HIGH BLOOD PRESSURE

Pay attention to your diet and relaxation and practise the following exercises daily:

- Sit for 10–20 minutes Watching your Breath (*see page 27*).
- Experiment with gentle Interrupted Breathing (*see page 119*).

  CAUTION: AVOID HEADSTAND, PURIFYING BREATH AND BELLOWS BREATH.

INSOMNIA

Try the following daily to promote relaxation, calm your body and induce sleep:

- Sit for 5–10 minutes Sealing Off Your Senses (*see page 141*) before bed.
- Cleanse blocked nasal passages with a neti pot (*see page 31*) before bed.
- As you lie in bed, practice 2:1 Breathing (*see page 51*).
- In the morning practice 3 rounds of Purifying Breath (*see page 32*).
- If new to breathing exercises, practise 10 rounds of Single Nostril Breathing, then of Simple Alternate Nostril Breathing (*see page 53*). After perfecting the latter, try 10 rounds of Alternate Nostril Breathing with a full retention (*see page 55*).
- Hold Plough Pose (*see page 147*) for as long as you feel comfortable. Follow with Fish Pose (*see page 101*), holding for half as long to release tension in your neck.

MEDITATION

Practising breath-awareness exercises is a good preparation for learning meditation techniques — try practising those recommended below daily. Also cleanse your respiratory system with a neti pot (*see page 31*) and at least 3 rounds of Purifying Breath (*see page 32*) every day:

- Sit in a meditative position (*see pages 35–7*) with your hands in Chin Mudra (*see page 34*), then spend 10–20 minutes Watching your Breath (*see page 27*).
- If new to breathing exercises, practise 10 rounds of Single Nostril Breathing, then of Simple Alternate Nostril Breathing (*see page 53*). After perfecting the latter, try 10 rounds of Alternate Nostril Breathing with a full retention (*see page 55*).
- Then begin to experiment with Box Breathing (*see page 91*).
- 5–10 minutes of Spinal Breathing (*see page 121*) or Sealing Off Your Senses (*see page 141*).
- Practise Headstand (*see page 103*) for 1–3 minutes before sitting to meditate.

MIGRAINES/HEADACHES

Breathing exercises can reduce pain and lessen the number of attacks. Cleanse daily with a neti pot (*see page 31*) and at least 3 rounds of Purifying Breath (*see page 32*). If you hyperventilate during a migraine, breathe into a paper bag for 30 seconds, rest, then repeat until your breathing is more regular. Try to do the following daily:

• If new to breathing exercises, practise 10 rounds of Single Nostril Breathing, then of Simple Alternate Nostril Breathing (*see page 53*). After perfecting the latter, try 10 rounds of Alternate Nostril Breathing with a full retention (*see page 55*).

• 3–5 minutes Sealing Off Your Senses (*see page 141*) and Interrupted Breathing (*see page 119*).

CAUTION: EXERCISES ARE PREVENTATIVE, DO NOT PRACTISE DURING A HEADACHE.

PREGNANCY/CHILDBIRTH

Read pages 114–15 and try at least one weekly pregnancy-yoga class. Explore the Lamaze Method, Bradley Method and Grantly Dick-Read Method and do this daily:

• Sit quietly for at least 10–20 minutes Watching Your Breath (*see page 27*) and/or spend 5–10 minutes Walking with your Breath (*see pages 92–3*).

• 10 repetitions of Single Nostril Breathing and Simple Alternate Nostril Breathing (*see page 53*).

• Sealing Off Your Senses (*see page 141*) and Bumblebee Breathing (*see page 139*).

• At least 2 rounds of Moon Salutation (*see page 122–7*).

CAUTION: AVOID ANY EXERCISES THAT INVOLVE PUMPING OR HOLDING YOUR BREATH, ABDOMINAL LIFT, ROOT AND CHIN LOCKS AND INVERTED POSES.

PRE-MENSTRUAL SYNDROME

Seven to ten days before menstruation, progesterone levels peak, causing carbon-dioxide levels in your blood to drop. If, like many people, you tend to hyperventiliate, your levels will already be low and the further drop can contribute to irritability, cramps, headaches and tiredness. At this time, practise the following daily:

• If new to breathing exercises, practise 10 rounds of Single Nostril Breathing, then of Simple Alternate Nostril Breathing (*see page 53*). After perfecting the latter, try 10 rounds of Alternate Nostril Breathing with a full retention (*see page 55*).

• Then begin to experiment with Box Breathing (*see page 91*).

• At least 2 rounds of Moon Salutation (*see page 122–7*). Continue to practise this sequence of poses during your menstrual period.

SPORTS PERFORMANCE

To use breathing to enhance your sports performance, begin by sitting for 10–20 minutes daily Watching Your Breath (*see page 27*). Cleanse your respiratory system with a neti pot (*see page 31*) and by practising at least 3 rounds of Purifying Breath (*see page 32*) daily. Add the following exercises to your training regime:

- If new to breathing exercises, practise 10 rounds of Single Nostril Breathing, then of Simple Alternate Nostril Breathing (*see page 53*). After perfecting the latter, try 10 rounds of Alternate Nostril Breathing with a full retention (*see page 55*).
- 6–12 rounds of Sun Salutation (*see pages 58–61*) followed by a 3–5 minute Headstand (*see page 103*) to enhance your balance and stamina.

STRESS

Try to remember the integral connection between feeling stressed, unhealthy breathing and poor posture. Read pages 110–13, then practise the Relaxation Breathing exercise on page 111. Feel free to experiment with any of the breathing exercises in this book, but try to practise the following daily:

- Sit for 10–20 minutes Watching your Breath (*see page 27*).
- If new to breathing exercises, practise 10 rounds of Single Nostril Breathing, then of Simple Alternate Nostril Breathing (*see page 53*). After perfecting the latter, try 10 rounds of Alternate Nostril Breathing with a full retention (*see page 55*).
- Open your chest with Fish Pose (*see page 101*).

WEIGHT PROBLEMS

The Prana and Samana Visualizations (*see pages 42–3 and 66–7*) can offer a healthy alternative to eating when you feel frustrated and/or anxious. It is important to cleanse your respiratory system using a neti pot (*see page 31*) and at least 3 rounds of Purifying Breath (*see page 32*) daily, then add the following into your daily routine:

- 6–12 Sun Salutation Sequences (*see pages 58–61*).
- Hold Shoulderstand (*see page 146*) for 1–3 minutes, Plough Pose (*see page 147*) for 2 minutes and Fish Pose (*see page 101*) for 1 minute.
- If new to breathing exercises, practise 10 rounds of Single Nostril Breathing, then of Simple Alternate Nostril Breathing (*see page 53*). After perfecting the latter, try 10 rounds of Alternate Nostril Breathing with a full retention (*see page 55*).
- Then add 5–10 rounds of Sun Breathing (*see page 71*).

GLOSSARY

AJNA: *sixth chakra; energy centre located between your eyebrows; the "third eye"; the brow chakra*

ALVEOLUS (plural: alveoli): *microscopic air sacs in your lungs where gaseous exchange takes place*

ANAHATA: *fourth chakra; energy centre located in the centre of your chest; the heart chakra*

APANA: *downward/outward-moving manifestation of prana; your cleansing breath*

BANDHA: *muscular lock applied by yogis during certain breathing and physical exercises*

BRONCHIAL TUBES: *two branches of the respiratory tube that carry air in and out of each lung*

CAPILLARY: *the smallest blood vessel in your body, its walls are one cell thick (i.e. microscopic) and porous, thus permitting the exchange of gases and nutrients*

CHAKRA: *subtle energy centre*

DIAPHRAGM: *the large muscle that causes you to breathe; separates chest from abdomen*

GASEOUS EXCHANGE: *when oxygen from the air you inhale passes into a capillary through the thin porous membranes of the alveolus and simultaneously carbon dioxide from your blood moves into the alveolus to be exhaled*

HATHA YOGA: *path of yoga that begins by working with the physical body, strengthening and purifying it with* asana *(physical exercises)*, pranayama *(breathing exercises) and* kriyas *(cleansing exercises). All facilitate purity of mind.*

HEMOGLOBIN: *protein in red blood cells that carries oxygen from your lungs to your cells*

IDA: *subtle energy channel, or nadi, located to the left of your spine*

INTERCOSTAL MUSCLES: *the muscles between your ribs; they move your ribs during the breathing process and aid your diaphragm*

KRIYA: *a yoga cleansing or purification exercise*

LARYNX: *voice box, located between your pharynx (throat) and trachea (windpipe); the cartridge at the front is referred to as the "Adam's apple"*

MANIPURA: *third chakra; energy centre located in your solar plexus region; the solar-plexus chakra*

MUDRA: *yoga exercises to "seal" your subtle energy; hand gestures*

MULADHARA: *first and lowest chakra; energy centre located at the base of your spine; the root chakra*

NADI: *subtle energy channel; equivalent to a meridian in acupuncture*

PHARYNX: *throat, the tube at the back of your nose and mouth that divides into the oesophagus (through which food travels) and larynx (through which air travels); it is considered a part of both your digestive and respiratory systems*

PINGALA: *subtle energy channel, or nadi, located to the right of your spine*

PRANA: *vital force; life energy; equivalent to the Chinese concept of chi and Japanese ki*

PRANAYAMA: *control of prana; the yogic science of breath control*

RESPIRATORY SYSTEM: *your body's breathing mechanism*

SAHASRARA: *seventh and highest chakra; energy centre located at the crown of your head; the crown chakra*

SAMANA: *digestive/balancing manifestation of prana; your nourishing breath*

SINUS: *facial cavity located behind your cheekbones and forehead*

SUSHUMNA: *the central nadi; approximates your spine*

TRACHEA: *the passageway for air between your larynx and bronchial tubes; your windpipe.*

UDANA: *upward "flying" manifestation of prana; your expressive breath*

VISUDDHA: *fifth chakra; energy centre located at your throat; the throat chakra*

VYANA: *the manifestation of prana that distributes energy; your expansive breath*

FURTHER READING

- Ambikananda, Swami, *Breathwork*, Thorsons, London & New York, 2001
- Desikachar, T.K.V., *The Heart of Yoga*, Inner Traditions, Vermont, 1995
- Frawley, David, *Yoga and Ayurveda*, Motilal Banarsidass, New Delhi, 2002
- Hale, Theresa; *Breathing Free*, Hodder & Stoughton, London, 1999; Mobius, New York, 2001
- Ivker, Robert S., *Asthma Survival*, Penguin Putnam, New York, 2001
- Iyengar, B.K.S., *Light on Pranayama*, Crossroad Publishing, New York, 2002
- Johari, Harish, *Breath, Mind and Consciousness*, Destiny Books, Vermont, 1989
- Kaminoff, Leslie, *Yoga Anatomy*, Human Kinetics, New York & London, 2007
- Lewis, Dennis, *The Tao of Natural Breathing*, Rodmell Press, Berkeley, 1997
- Muktibodhananda Saraswati, Swami, *Swara Yoga*, Bihar School of Yoga, Mungar, 1983
- Niranjanananda, Swami, *Prana, Pranayama, Prana Vidya*, Yoga Publications Trust, Bihar, 1994
- Rama, Swami, *Science of Breath*, The Himalayan Institute Press, Pennsylvania, 1979
- Rosen, Richard, *Yoga of Breath*, Shambala, Boston, 2002
- Saradananda, Swami, *Chakra Meditation*, Duncan Baird Publishers, London & New York, 2008
- Spreads, Carola, *Ways to Better Breathing*, Healing Arts Press, Vermont, 1978
- Tuli-Dinsmore, Uma, *Mother's Breath*, Sitaram and Sons, London, 2006
- Van Lysebeth, Andre, *Pranayama: the Yoga of Breathing*, Unwin Paperbacks, London, 1979
- Vishnu-devananda, Swami, *Complete Illustrated Book of Yoga*, Crown Publishers, New York, 1960
- Vishnu-devananda, Swami, ed., *Hatha Yoga Pradipika*, OM Lotus Publishing, New York, 1987
- Weil, Andrew, *Breathing: The Master Key to Self Healing*, Sounds True, Colorado, 1999

FURTHER RESOURCES

- **Alexander Technique** www.stat.org.uk: releases tension by re-educating your breathing.
- **Anapanasati "mindfulness of breathing"** www.audiodharma.org/talks-anapanasati.html: Buddhist meditation set out in *Anapanasati Sutra*.
- **Art of Living Foundation** www.artofliving.org: Sri Sri Ravi Shankar's simple breathing practices.
- **Autogenic Training** www.autogenic-therapy.org: verbal relaxation commands to control breathing.
- **Bioenergetics** www.bionenergetictherapy.com: using breath to overcome "muscle armouring".
- **Buteyko Method** www.buteyko.co.uk: breathing techniques to relieve repiratory symptoms.
- **Conscious Breathing:** technique with many well-known teachers – search online for one near you.
- **Dennis Lewis** www.dennislewis.org: the work of the author of The Tao of Natural Breathing.
- **Gurdjieff** www.gurdjieff.org: psycho-spiritual transformation with a focus on breathing.
- **Holotropic Breathwork** www.holotropic.com: psychotherapeutic approach to breathing.
- **Martial Arts:** investigate the approach to breathing in Akido, Karate, Qi Gong and Tai Chi.
- **Rebirthing-Breathwork** www.rebirthing breathwork.co.uk: conscious, connected breathing aka Intuitive or Conscious Energy Breathing.
- **Taoist Healing Breath** www.healing-tao.co.uk: practice of Chi Nei Tank, International Healing Tao
- **Yoga:** investigate Swami Ramdev (www.swamiramdevyoga.com), ICYER (International Centre of Yoga Education and Research; www.icyer.com), Satyananda yoga (www.syclondon.com), Sivananda yoga (www.sivananda.org), T.K.V. Desikachar's viniyoga (www.kym.org).

INDEX

ACKNOWLEDGMENTS

PICTURE CREDITS
22 From *Subtle Body: Essence and Shadow*
by David V. Tansley, Thames & Hudson Ltd.,
London and New York

AUTHOR'S ACKNOWLEDGMENTS
Thanks to Kelly Thompson, who inspired this book
and got the project off the ground. I have incorporated
the five prana visualizations from Dr David Frawley's
Yoga and Ayurveda into my classes: they provide much
of the motivation behind this book.

Swami Saradananda can be contacted via her website
at: www.FlyingMountainYoga.org

PUBLISHER'S ACKNOWLEDGMENTS
The publisher would like to thank:
Model: Sarina, MOT Models
Make-up artist: Justine Martin